THE WORK OF HER HANDS

THE
Work
OF HER
Hands

A prairie woman's life in remembrances and recipes

A memoir by
Plynn Gutman

POPLAR
PRESS

Published in Canada by Poplar Press, a division of Wolsak and Wynn Publishers Ltd., Hamilton.

Cover design: Julie McNeill, McNeill Design Arts
Author's photograph: Mitchell Gutman
Typeset in Utopia
Printed by Ball Media, Brantford, Canada

The publisher gratefully acknowledges the support of the Canada Council for the Arts, the Ontario Arts Council and the Book Publishing Industry Development Program (BPIDP) for their financial assistance.

The Canada Council | Le Conseil des Arts
for the Arts | du Canada

Poplar Press
69 Hughson Street North, Ste 102
Hamilton, ON
Canada L8R 1G5
www.wolsakandwynn.ca

ONTARIO ARTS COUNCIL
CONSEIL DES ARTS DE L'ONTARIO

Canadian   Patrimoine
Heritage   canadien

Library and Archives Canada Cataloguing in Publication

Gutman, Plynn
    The work of her hands : a prairie woman's life in remembrances and recipes / by Plynn Gutman.

Includes index.

ISBN 978-1-894987-51-6

1. Lacaille, Marie-Anne, 1902-2000. 2. Frontier and pioneer life–Saskatchewan. 3. Saskatchewan–Biography. I. Title.

FC3523.1.L33A3 2010   971.24'02092   C2010-903446-5

In memory of my grandmother
Marie-Anne Lacaille

Her quick, old hands, the steady, even rhythm of her work sunk deep into my memory, planting seeds of thought, the beginnings of questions that I did not know how to ask until life had carried me a while – like a dandelion seed floating in a prairie breeze until it finally drops and takes root.

Contents

No mens

It was a "no mens" party, a term lovingly coined after a phrase my maternal grandmother, Marie-Anne Lacaille, sometimes used. "We don't need no mens," she would say, her French-Canadian accent lingering in the intonation of her voice, not with malice or condescension but rather with strength of conviction. She was of the mind that women were quite able to manage with or without their mens – something she accomplished quite adeptly over the course of her life. My grandmother looked tiny, yet regal, in the black chiffon dress she had chosen for the occasion, her hair coiffed in perfect snow-coloured curls with delicate white earrings on her lobes. She was sitting with ankles demurely crossed in the not-so-big blue velvet armchair of the hotel suite we rented for the party. Her cheeks blushed as she laughed, a small chuckle on the verge of a giggle. She seemed both uncomfortable and pleased with all the attention.

I am trying to remember why we planned the celebration that way. Maybe it was because five years before, the entire clan, including her children, their spouses and all of the grandkids – seventy-six of us – held a ninetieth birthday celebration for her, and to do it again would have seemed anticlimactic. Or maybe it was that, at ninety-five, we thought the dinner-dance-party atmosphere would be too much for her, as she would insist on having a whisky with water, or two, and dancing every dance until the evening ended. But really, I think we just wanted her to ourselves.

All eyes were on her as she opened her birthday gifts – silly gifts, simple gifts. Like the giant jar of Cheez Whiz, which she loved spread thick on her morning toast, or the bucket of saskatoons, the kind of wild berries she used to pick from stands of brush on the Saskatchewan farm and then eat, by the bowlful, splattered with a light coat of heavy cream she'd separated from that morning's milk-ing. But it was the teddy bear that pleased her most. As a child growing up on a prairie homestead, she'd never had one of her own. All available hands worked the farm in one way or the other, with little time set aside for the whimsy of children's play. When she opened the box that held the bear, her eyes glittered with tears. A tiny frown on my grandmother's forehead, pulled into place by raised eyebrows, seemed mismatched with the wide smile on her ruby painted lips. She hugged the bear tightly, its black nose nestled next to the corsage pinned to her chest as if taking in the carnation's musty-sweet scent, then relaxed her hold and cradled it as she would a small child.

She had held each of us – her three daughters, six of her grand-daughters and three of her great-granddaughters – in the same way, her hands always warm, her touch gentle. We watched her, smiling and remembering. Each of us had our own special memories of times spent with her. In that moment I was eight years old again: sitting with her while she rocked back and forth in her easy chair, eyes closed, fingering her rosary; or curled up next to her on her bed, the cool of the flowered spread beneath me, my head on the crocheted pillowslip and holding her hand, warm and strong, its skin diaphanous and delicate. Listening to her soft snore and then, too, falling into a secure, dreaming sleep.

I'm not sure any of us realized then how she had become our touchstone, an example of the way we live as women in this world. Now, when I observe myself, my mother, my sisters, all my female relatives, I see her in all of us – hardworking, determined, loyal women, creative and adaptable, but just a little bit stubborn; women easy with laughter, and with tears.

She fondled one of the teddy bear's legs, rubbing the soft fur back and forth, touching it lightly with her fingertips, like pushing a tiny pillow. A certain nimbleness remained in her hands though the knuckles were slightly swollen and the skin almost translucent over bumpy, blue veins. She used one hand to gather a tissue from her lap and daintily wiped her nose, which was dripping from laughing and crying. That was my grandmother's way – laughing and crying at the same time, sometimes with grace, sometimes with passion.

Tranche

Most of my relatives from both sides of the family have farmed the grain fields of southern Saskatchewan since the early 1900s. Many still do. Their farms, now in the care of second or third generations, have changed little from those early days. In the yards, shiny metal silos may have replaced rows of wood granaries, but the original barns and tool sheds likely remain. Some are still in use as they have been for decades, often repainted in traditional red, while others are left to sag into slow decay, the wood, brittle and weathered to a solemn grey. Many of the original one- or two-storey homestead houses are also standing, with their cellars once used as cold storage for food. My grandmother's childhood home that housed a family of thirteen is now used to store paint, lumber and old furniture. Farmers are frugal and creative in their use of everything, including buildings. Too, I think the old ones – even those sagging into the earth – are kept as icons of past generations' hard work. All the farms still have big earthen plots for vegetable gardens in yards that are bordered by rows of trees to break the bold, prairie wind. When you drive along the highway, these stands of poplars and pines dot the flat fields like oases offering pleasant relief from the rigors of working the land.

As a small child in the 1950s, our farmyard was my entire existence, a busy yet lonely place. I spent long hours trailing behind my mother as she did a giant list of house and yard chores or, when the weather was fine, silently making mud pies on an old, wood table in the corner of the yard while she tended the vegetable garden. We'd both be waiting to hear the sound of bicycle wheels crumbling gravel and the chatter of my sisters' and brothers' voices, as they neared the end of their two-mile bike ride from school in Amulet. Amulet, now gone and memorialized by a roadside cairn, was the local farming community's hub situated next to the CPR line; a small town, supposedly named by a railroad official who found a small jewel on a temporary train platform in 1910.

My siblings – Elaine, Sylvia, Edward and Robert (better known as Bob) – looked a little like nesting dolls, the way the sizes of their bikes decreased with their ages. Elaine, the oldest and twelve years my senior, of course had the biggest bike, down to Bob, five years older than me, who had a tiny one with balloon tires; his eight-year-old legs had to peddle furiously to keep up with the others. Though they had chores and school work to do when they got home, their presence at least changed the quiet for a time.

During the winter, when the snow piled several feet deep, too deep for travel by car, my father took my brothers and sisters to school by horse and sleigh. He would return home to do his chores and then go back to town to play cards at the general store with some of the neighbouring farmers until school let out. Sometimes I'd accompany him on these afternoon trips, a little change from staying indoors watching my mother sew clothes or braid rugs. I have a dream-like memory of standing amongst shelves of canned goods eating chocolate-covered malted milk balls from a box and watching my father deal cards to several men at a table next to a big wood stove. Its radiating heat cloaks the air. In full winter gear – a heavy coat with leggings and a matching bonnet my mother made for me – I am sweating, the malted balls melting in my hand, the chocolate, sickly sweet in my mouth.

So many of my memories of those years are related to food, especially the preparation of big meals. My grandparents, most of our relatives and my parents' good friends lived a few miles or an easy Sunday's drive away from us, so we often gathered after church to relax, visit and, of course, eat. For the women this meant a great deal of work but it also offered a change from the long weekdays that kept them isolated on the farm – all the talking and laughing amidst pans clattering in the kitchen. The men stayed clear of the meal preparations, busying themselves with talking and smoking cigarettes. And us kids played quietly until we were all called to dinner to watch the grand procession of the women brushing against one another in the bustle of putting food on the dinner table. Everyone waited with approving grins for the great pleasure of passing dishes, tasting food well-prepared. The solitary nature of those quiet week-days quickly disappeared.

Mostly the meals were huge, if not elaborate, especially in the summer when vegetables from the garden were plentiful. Along with fried chicken and maybe cold, sliced ham, we'd have boiled new potatoes, green and yellow beans, fresh peas, cooked beets in a splash of vinegar and a tower of corn on the cob. Not to mention plates stacked with raw carrots, radishes and spring onions, and a big round bowl of leaf lettuce tossed with sour cream and vinegar. But one of my favourite meals was a simple dish my grandmother used to make – *tranche*, pronounced by rolling the tongue over the "t" and "r," landing heavily in an "ah" and sliding out with a "shh" sound, which in French means "slice." In this case, thin slices of potatoes, cooked directly on the smooth iron top of a coal stove; a one-item meal she, as a young wife and mother, served her family in the direst days of the Great Depression.

My grandmother was a master at making something wonder-fully delicious out of almost nothing. But if you told her this she'd shrug her shoulders and pucker her lips as if they were forming the word *jour* – her French-Canadian way of expressing nonchalance – and say, "Well, we just make do with what we have."

My mother recalls differently, "Oh, we all loved it when Mom made tranche. It was a treat. We didn't care if we had anything else – just those little, burnt slices of potato soaked in butter … the butter made them taste so good."

Yes, so good. Addicting. Like potato chips. As with so many of my grandmother's recipes, this dish remained a family favourite, which she continued to serve even in more prosperous times, as did my mother. We had an old, coal stove sitting in the yard near the house on the farm for just that purpose. But when we moved to the city, we had all the modern, electrical conveniences and no coal stove in sight. Our tranche meals were few. Unless my father, who also adored the dish, used his salesman's savvy as a farm implement dealer to sway an unsuspecting rural relative or one of his customer's wives, who still had a working coal stove, into letting my mother cook up a ten-pound batch in exchange for a bottle of whisky or a good deal on a tractor. Embarrassed, she would comply only because she missed the dish even more than he did.

On a few occasions I've tried to recreate the recipe using a pancake griddle. It hints at the experience, but it doesn't truly capture it. I know it's because eating tranche was never just about the potatoes. Over the years it became a ritual of memory and experience. Without fail, after a few bites, my elder relatives would start to tell stories about how good a meal of potatoes tasted even when the previous night's meal was potatoes, and the next night's would be, too. Or they would reminisce about the time lightning struck the house, or what it was like when the rain finally came again.

I remember one such meal in our yard, with everyone gathered around card tables covered with my mother's hand-embroidered cloths. My grandfather sits sideways in a fold-out chair, one arm draped over the back, the other leaning on the table, "Sacamogee," he says (no one ever knew what this meant, but over time our family agreed that it was his own, personal cuss word), "them was hard times, real hard times." My father nods as he chews, his bottom lip glistening with butter.

I can see my grandmother standing at that old, coal stove, an apron tied around her waist, one hand on her hip, the other poking and testing the pieces. The permed curls of her brown hair are brushed away from her face, which still has a soft smoothness to it even in her fifties. Her lips stretch over her straight, white teeth in a radiant smile. Back then I didn't know that she wore dentures and had done so for many years. My mother tells me she had been plagued with toothaches all of her life, her teeth slowly, painfully rotting away. The dentist offered to take out a few at a time, but she bluntly said, "No. Take them all out. Get it over with." So at the age of thirty-nine, just a few months before my mother married my father, she had all of them pulled in one agonizing experience. That way she'd have "good teeth" for the wedding.

"Oh, Eddie," I hear my mother say as she ferries a hot bowl of potatoes in pot-holdered hands to the table, while my brothers jockey for their next helpings. My father has no doubt told one of his many jokes that I am too young to understand. My mother and grandmother are laughing, the same open-mouthed expression, the sound falling somewhere between a giggle and a guffaw, contagious and full. I laugh, too, as I eat my tranche, warm, chewy and delightfully buttery in my mouth, while a breeze shimmers the leaves of the poplar trees into a thousand tiny lights in the last stretch of the setting sun.

Our way of being together as a family has not changed over the years, though now many of us live much further away from each other than an easy Sunday's drive. So when we do gather, we find that many of our best times are around a table, sharing good food and often reflecting on the past, like our parents and grandparents did. We like to linger over last sips of wine – our stomachs, round and satisfied – and engage in great political debates or philosophical discussions on values, life. Some of us lean in with elbows on the table, trying to talk over one another; others sit back with arms folded across chests, listening, ruminating. All of this is part of our family repartee. And often after that, as was the custom in my grandparents' home, we will play cards late into the evening – cajoling or reprimanding one another about our game-playing skills – and nibble on cookies and mixed nuts though we've all just sworn after dinner that we might never eat again. We like meals that are events and take hours, not minutes; long communions that keep us close after we've parted; big family meals held strong by our Old World heritage.

I haven't tasted tranche in many years, and today I am a long way from that place I still call home. The Sonoran Desert of Arizona, where I have lived now for nearly twenty-five years, is very different – being this far south, of course, distinctly changes the topography and natural vegetation. However, they do have some similarities. The summer heat in Arizona and winter cold of the prairies keep you indoors and out of the elements. And there are a few days here in October, when the weather begins to turn, when the scents of alyssum and petunias in my garden mix and linger in the warm, fresh air and the sun hangs in the blue sky between soft clumps of white clouds, and they feel like those special summer days of my youth.

I've been thinking: why couldn't I find an old, coal stove and set it in my yard just as my parents did? Hardly different from the fancy, patio firepits we have these days to sit around with our cocktails and hors d'oeuvres. I could buy a couple of ten-pound bags of potatoes when they go on sale at the grocery store – frugality is a natural consequence of being a child of the children of the Great Depression – and I could have a tranche party. It would mean spending several hours cutting potatoes into ultra-thin slices while building a nice fire in the stove, and then standing over it for an hour or two tending to the cooking; poking and lifting each delicate slice at one edge to check if it is brown and toasty enough to turn over; and slowly filling a giant bowl warming on the corner of the stove.

Yes, I could serve those beautiful, thin slices, coated in organic, melted butter, with a crisp, white wine and a big, romaine salad. And we – my family and a few close friends who appreciate my idiosyncrasies – could sit in my desert yard and eat and talk and laugh just like we used to, like generations before us did. And as the scent of alyssum and petunias floats on the breeze, maybe this would hold me, hold all of us, a bit closer to a time we are forgetting and revive our memories of the people and the land that have shaped us.

TRANCHE

10 pounds of potatoes (approximately)
1/4 to 1/2 pound butter
Salt and pepper, to taste

A nice, hot fire in a coal stove works best for this dish.

Peel potatoes and slice lengthwise at a thickness of 1/4 inch or less. Put slices directly on top of the stove and sprinkle with salt. Brown on one side, then turn over and brown the other. When done, put pieces in a warm bowl on the corner of the stove. Repeat process with next batch of pieces.

When cooking is completed, melt desired amount of butter in a pan, then pour over potato slices and toss. Sprinkle with salt and pepper, and serve.

Like most women of her time, my grandmother used a McClary cook stove on the farm. It was designed to burn coal but during the Depression she used whatever she could – coal, wood, even dried cow-pies. She fed the stove's fire through a small latched door in its bottom left-hand corner, and the main baking oven opened just right of its centre. On the smooth, flat top of the stove she kept handy her black, iron pot for cooking meat and a kettle for boiling water. A big, round pipe at the rear of the stove ran up along a heat guard before it elbowed out the wall of the kitchen to the chimney. A shelf shouldered the pipe at the top of the stove, where enough heat generated to keep some dishes warm while she prepared others. My grandmother liked to tell a story about that stove pipe.

A summer storm had been building, thunder crackling off in the distance. She was busy in the kitchen, and my mother, Florence, about eight years old at the time, was reading, sitting in a chair nearby. My grandmother said, "I want her to help me with the chores, but she just ignore me." My mother kept reading one more page and then another until my grandmother began to lose her temper, "I say to her, 'you better get over here and help me right now, or you get a spanking!'" With this, my mother reluctantly put down her book and rose from the chair.

Not five minutes later, lightning struck the chimney. The current ran in the house through the stove to the very chair my mother had occupied and ignited a fire. My grandmother fiercely fought it, pounding the flames with rags until my grandfather appeared. By a strange coincidence, he had witnessed the strike, saw smoke rising from the farmyard and bolted in from the field to find out what had been hit. Had he not come to her aid the house and their few possessions would have been lost. None of which really mattered to my grandmother. She told this story often over her lifetime, with a certain awe and disgust. Her daughter had been miraculously saved; but on the other hand, look how close she had come to death, as if somehow God had gambled with her child's life.

The sweet breath of memory

My mother and I huddled together at my computer in a little alcove of my family room, mulling over measurements and oven temperatures in our attempt to reconstruct my grandmother's recipes. It was a couple of years after my grandmother had passed on and we still missed her terribly. She had been a marvellous cook. Her dinner table was the centre of many of our best memories of her, and we wanted something tangible to keep her spirit alive. It seems that when someone lives a long life, as she did into her ninety-seventh year, with a great deal of spunk and verve, a cord of immortality wraps gently around that person and those who love her. You begin to think, she'll be with us for another year, and another ... and then another after that. So when the end does come and the cord unravels, the disconnection feels ominous.

In the alcove of my family room, my mother and I, Marie-Anne Lacaille's eldest child and tenth grandchild, began trying to reconnect that cord through her recipes. Some, my mother called out from memory just as my grandmother would have; others, she read to me from her well-used, brown, spiral notebook. The hurried scrawls were no doubt written while my mother leaned on a kitchen counter watching her mother's quick hands, because my grandmother never wrote down any of her recipes. She learned to cook by observing and, I think, if there ever was a time when she could have written them down, she was already too connected to the intuitive nature of her cooking to do so. She knew the look of the measure of flour needed to make pie crust; the feel of the batter's thickness when she stirred a batch of oatmeal cookies; the subtle taste of spices combined in the meat of her tourtière; the smell of baked bread ready to take out of the oven. She was too accustomed to cooking this way to ruin the rhythm of her work by chronicling a cup of this and a half teaspoon of that. Besides, though she never said so, I think she was somewhat of the mind that if you wanted to learn you watched and then you tried, just as she had done.

As my mother and I muddled along trying to piece together our memories of her stirring and pouring, and craft written recipes out of her bits of this and pinches of that, a picture of my grandmother, one that I had not seen clearly before, started to emerge.

My grandmother's recipes are the icons of her life – from her birthplace in Quebec to her family's homestead in southern Saskatchewan; from her years on the prairies during the Great Depression to some of the many places she lived in her later years. Though they are simple recipes, reflective of earlier times, they taste deeply delicious, as if infused with the rich history out of which they were born. When I prepare and taste them I revisit my grandmother's life and can relate more deeply to the comfort and rhythm, the courage and even the despair of her experiences. My memory of her continues, a sweet, warm breath whispering in my ear.

They called us pea-soupers

My grandmother's birthdate was July 27, 1902. She was the eleventh of thirteen children born to Ferdinand and Philomène Fradette in the county of Bellechasse, located just south of the St. Lawrence River, in Quebec. One of my cousins traced our family back to the late 1600s and a young man, Jean Fradet, from Marsillac, a town in the old Guyenne province of France. No one knows what prompted him, at the age of twenty-two, to leave the French countryside to build a life in the cold, wooded wilderness of New France. But the generations that followed – Augustin, Jean-Baptiste, Joseph, Pierre, his namesake Pierre and Ferdinand – turned out families of farmers as courageous and forward-thinking as young Jean must have been back then.

Ferdinand, my great-grandfather, owned a long strip of land in Bellechasse, one end bordering a creek, lush with sugar maples they tapped for syrup. But, with eight sons, he had no opportunity to expand his estate since the population was too dense and additional farmland, not available. So in the early 1900s, when the Federal Government began offering homesteads in the West, my great-grandfather decided to stake claims for his sons and himself in what was called Canada's new frontier. There, he believed he could build a family dynasty in a way that Quebec could not offer. Clifford Sifton, the minister of the interior, welcomed settlers like my great-grandfather: hard-working people who wanted their children and grandchildren to carry on the homesteads and permanently populate the land.

Like Jean Fradet six generations before him, Ferdinand traded the known for the unknown and made a trip to southern

Saskatchewan with his eldest son, Joseph, to secure his piece of the prairies. By late 1910 he had claimed several quarter-sections of land a few miles south of the small town of Radville. And in the early months of 1911 the entire family, in addition to livestock and lumber for farm buildings, travelled by train to the raw, unbroken land. First Nations peoples had once roamed the area but now only gophers and rabbits made their homes in the rich, black earth, while a host of meadowlarks and chickadees, crows and brown sparrows foraged the tall, mixed grass or scrub bush for food. My grandmother, Marie-Anne, was eight years old.

I wonder what it was like for her to leave the deep green of forests, the orange and umber fall maples, only to step off the train after weeks of weary travel into the bald, winter-white land where one could look toward the horizon and see nothing but a long, thin, pencil line dividing the heavens from the earth. And, for the first six months after arriving, the entire Fradette family lived in a one-room house. During the day the boys moved the beds outside into the yard so the house could serve as a kitchen and eating area. At night they moved them indoors once again, lined up in tight rows, where the family slept three and maybe four to each bed. A table and chairs took their place under a milky sweep of stars in the cloudless, prairie sky. No one had any privacy except behind the raised lid of a trunk, off to one side of the room, where each took his or her turn washing or dressing.

They say the land was full of promises and big plans back then; promises made by the government, if only they would come and work the land. Like every push into the frontier, homesteaders hoped not only to sustain themselves but also to prosper, imagining substantial cash returns from harvested wheat and rye. But just getting to the point of planting seed required long, hard days for everyone, including children. Each had his or her chores and plenty of them. The Fradette boys helped their father break the land and build sheds and the two-storey house they so badly needed. The older girls, Marie and Marilda, helped their mother in the kitchen. My grandmother saw little of the work and flow of meal preparations as she and Audelie, fifteen months her senior, were in charge of yard chores and milking cows. She only spent time in the kitchen cranking the handle of the milk separator or tending to the meticulous cleaning of its many parts.

And beyond the arduous farm work, prejudice muddled its way into their lives. The local Anglo population, many only once or twice removed from their own immigration, was dubious about the influx of French Canadians. Saskatchewan, in the years that led up to its formation and provincial inauguration in 1905, had been promoted as a British province, the first settlers recruited purposefully from Ontario and England. However, many of these settlers, whose sensibilities leaned toward a more genteel culture, could not, or chose not, to endure the rigors of prairie life, which prompted the government to expand its homesteading invitation to other ethnicities and countries. Ferdinand Fradette and his family had accepted this invitation. But the French, who came from Canada (mostly Quebec), the United States and Belgium, made up only five percent of the immigrant population in the entire province. The small cluster of these settlers south of Radville was very aware of its minority status.

"We didn't speak no English." My grandmother paused, took a deep breath. "At school we got put with the little ones. The ones our age teased us because we were so big. They thought we were stupid, but we had to learn English, you see ... and the teacher, she never said nothing to stop them."

She was speaking of Audelie and herself, both several years older than the Anglo six-year-olds learning the same reading and writing skills in the one-room schoolhouse.

"But they teased our brothers, too. Emile and Henri, they weren't big."

During such recollections my grandmother would often fall silent, her hands folded in her lap, looking away, watching distant moments only visible to her. She had a habit of rubbing the back of one hand with the thumb of the other, moving her aging skin into gentle folds, then stretching it back to a youthful smoothness. I think now, this was the habit of someone used to having busy hands.

"They called us 'pea-soupers' ..." she said, her voice trailing off, "yes ... that was hard on us. It make us feel bad."

The Soda Lake School was two miles down the road from the Fradette home, a rectangular wood building sitting on the rise of a hill by a dirt road. A couple of years ago I visited the old school, now long abandoned to the modern one in Radville, some twelve miles north. I was taken aback by the smallness of it. How difficult it would have been for children to learn in such close quarters, how large a scolding from the teacher must have felt, how loud a mean whisper would have sounded.

Marie-Anne and Audelie only attended school for three years, which provided them with basic skills in reading, writing and speaking English. My grandmother's school experience was demoralizing, but she enjoyed learning and probably would have continued her education even in the midst of discrimination if she and her sister hadn't had to care for the cows above all else.

Every day, in good weather and bad, morning and evening, they took a horse and wagon out to the pasture where they coaxed the cows into milking. The two of them would sit huddled together on the rough plank of wood at the wagon's head in the dim light of dawn; the reins hanging loose in my grandmother's hands while a soft clucking sound slipped from her lips – the click of the tongue at the back of the throat – urging the horse on. And then in the pasture, they called the cows, "Coboss, coboss." No one can tell me what coboss means or how it came to be used, but the sound and its magical response are as clear to me now as in my own childhood, when my mother called our cattle in from the pasture. I remember the cows, as if in a trance, would begin to appear upon the rise of land – one, then two, and then the gathering of the small herd sauntering slowly towards us chewing their cuds in a lazy sideways motion. A child of three or four, I always stood close to my mother, tucked under her arm, her hand about my shoulder, just a little afraid. The warmth of her touch and the faint sweetness of her perspiration made me feel safe as the big, bony animals lumbered past us toward the barn, plopping loose, green pies and swishing their tails.

I suppose there was no time for my grandmother or her sister to be afraid of cows. I can see them there in the field sitting on their three-legged stools, separated by a respectable distance to keep their cows calm, and bent low beneath the bellies whish-whooshing long streams of milk into metal pails. The musky-sweet scent of grass heavy with dew rises in a push of prairie breeze. Maybe, while they work, they practice singing a duet for next Sunday's social gathering. Or sometimes, after the evening milking, once they have transferred the pails of warm, fresh milk into five-gallon cans sitting on the wagon bed, they might linger for a while and watch the cows meander away until they become silhouettes on the burnished horizon. They could not have been eager to return home to the long process of separating the milk from the cream. Except on harsh winter days:

the crunch of frozen snow beneath their feet; cold hands squeezing cold teats; milk throwing steam from the pail as if from a pot on a hot stove.

Despite their age difference, Marie-Anne and Audelie seemed like twins. Most pictures show them together: two stoic, young girls, sometimes with hair coiffed, in Sunday dresses and laced, heeled boots, but mostly in the plain clothes of workers, sleeves rolled up, aprons soiled. One shows them by the house, as if stopping only for a moment and the click of the camera, busy on their way to their chores; another, by the wagon and team of horses, perhaps on the way to milking.

"We only had each other, you know," my grandmother told me.

I think this was her way of saying that the two of them had formed a childhood alliance to survive their hardships. How difficult the adjustment to prairie life must have been with its unyielding and unending chores. Together they braved the undercurrent of discrimination in the community and clung to each other against the domineering, difficult nature of their father and, like him, their older brothers.

"We work like dogs," she would recall often, many years later, shaking her head, the words tinged with bitterness, "like damned dogs."

She spoke, too, with a certain sadness and regret for her mother, Philomène, a small, somewhat frail woman who bore thirteen children, clothed and fed them and ran the household alone when Ferdinand left for months at a time each winter to visit Quebec. Philomène, who always welcomed him back with open arms, graciously accepting the jugs of maple syrup he brought with him, a small appeasement for his absence.

I could find only a few photographs of my great-grandmother. In one, as a child of maybe ten years, she stands with her twin sister holding hands in a formal pose, the two looking uncannily like Audelie and Marie-Anne, their features dark, their eyes focused in a distant stare. In another, Philomène stands with her husband and eleven of their children in front of the two-storey house on the Saskatchewan farm. She wears a light, high-collared blouse, the sleeves rolled to her elbows, with a long, dark skirt; she is taller than her two youngest sons, Emile and Henri, but Marie-Anne – probably about twelve and petite in her own right – is already her height. Maybe I imagine it, but I see weariness in her deep-set eyes and resignation (or is that determination?) in the downturn of her mouth.

Over the years my grandmother often reflected on the plight of women during that time. The French-Canadian culture was distinctly patriarchal – a society of men who liked to drink homebrew and smoke cigars while their women waited on them, quiet and accommodating. From her stories I built up a picture of those times.

"Marie-Anne, fetch another jug."

"Come on, you'll never catch a man moving that slow."

A slap on her hind end as she passes. A thunder of raucous laughter.

This order of things never sat well with my grandmother. When they were teenagers, she and Audelie conspired to run away. It was their attempt at emancipation. No more milking cows, no more chores day and night. They turned to a neighbour, Mrs. Forshee, for help.

Several years earlier Mrs. Forshee had saved the Fradette family from being wiped out by scarlet fever. An epidemic, the fever had spread like a raging prairie fire; everyone except Ferdinand and one child, Napoléon, was ill. It started with a sore throat, then a skin rash and fever so high that several of them lost their hair. Philomène was so sick there were whispers that she might be lost to the fever. At eleven years old, baldheaded and barely recovered herself, Marie-Anne sat vigil with Audelie at their mother's bedside until she was well.

Mrs. Forshee left her husband and seven children for many days in order to care for the family, tend to their sore throats with warm broth, their fevers with cold cloths, and scrape their white tongues with a spoon. I found a photograph of her in a book by the Radville Laurier Historical Society, which chronicles the history of the Radville area and its people. Viola Forshee stands next to her husband, her brow creased and eyes squinting from behind wire-rimmed glasses on a cloudless, prairie day. She looks to be a formidable woman, as tall as her husband, lean, and with the presence and stature of a man – her arms, long and her feet, sizable in the leather boots that protrude from beneath her full skirt. Though she spoke only English, and the Fradettes only French, her fearlessness and compassion during that time spoke clearly enough. With the worry brought on by the epidemic and the thought of losing their mother, both Marie-Anne and Audelie drew close to her and visited her often thereafter.

So surely on the day the two sisters decided to take flight they believed that Mrs. Forshee would understand and could help them find a way to leave, maybe go to the city – to Regina – where they would find jobs and live on their own.

They would have knocked on her door, hand-in-hand, and when Mrs. Forshee opened it to them, I'm sure the look on her face was not one of surprise but rather a questioning smile, small and grim.

"My dears, what brings you all this way in the middle of the day?"

Audelie spoke first. "We … we've come to ask for your help, Mrs. Forshee."

"Is someone sick?"

They hesitated, looked at one another. My grandmother took a deep breath, "No, Mrs. Forshee. We … my sister and me … we have run away, and … and we never want to go back."

She ushered them into the house, sat them at the rough-hewn wood table in the kitchen and let them tell their woes – Audelie spoke fast and passionately, Marie-Anne added details to her stories, while Mrs. Forshee shook her head and tisked between unsmiling lips. But then, before she could put a plan into action, and without a doubt the girls were certain she had one, their father knocked at the door.

In their innocence, the girls were shocked that he had found them. But, in truth, their discovery was inevitable. The Forshee farm was the only one for miles around that did not belong to one of their relatives or older brothers, and the French community was close and loyal. Had anyone seen the girls on their trek, they would have aided Ferdinand in his search.

He entered the Forshee home in long, confident strides, his back stiff, the tipping of his hat, formal. He was authoritative as always but acted kindly in front of Mrs. Forshee, chuckling as if the incident was some humorous mistake. She, in turn, said little except, "Girls, you're welcome to visit me any time you like," her words slow and deliberate as she looked straight into their father's face.

I expect that my grandmother and Audelie left Mrs. Forshee as they had arrived, hand-in-hand, their alliance intact; that they climbed into the wagon and rode in silence back to the farm, stealing glances at one another but keeping their eyes far away from their father's.

PEA SOUP

3 cups dried yellow peas
Salt and pepper, to taste
A ham bone or a 3 inch by 3 inch piece of salt pork
1 medium onion, chopped

Wash peas thoroughly and drain in a colander. Soak peas in a bowl of water overnight.

When ready to cook, put peas and soaking water in a large pot on the stove. Add salt and pepper, bone or meat and onion. Add more water to cover and bring to a boil. Reduce heat and simmer for 3 hours, stirring often. Remove bone. If peas are not mushy, mash them with a potato masher. Serve.

French-Canadian food evolved from the early days of New France and its population of explorers, hunters and trappers, who ate a meat-based diet filled with lots of hearty soups and stews that could nourish them and their families through the long months of winter. A cast iron pot served as the main cooking utensil, a durable kettle that could hang over the flames of a log fire. Generations of women continued to use an iron pot, which is known more commonly now as a Dutch oven. My grandmother used hers to create many savoury dishes, first on a coal stove and later on an electric one. Pea soup provided a great cold weather meal that stuck to your ribs and warmed your insides.

As a result of the huge population growth in Quebec, which left thousands of farmers landless and unable to find affordable, accessible and fertile land, many French Canadians migrated south to the United States and west into Canada's frontier in search of a better life. The less-than-kind nickname "pea-soupers" identified these brave souls.

MAPLE SYRUP TAFFY

A jug of maple syrup
A fresh snowbank

If a fresh bank is not available, use an existing one by brushing old or dirty snow away to expose clean snow. Pour one thin strip of maple syrup, approximately 6 to 8 inches long, into the snow for each person in your party. Let sit for a few minutes.

Then let everyone pull a strip out of the snow with their thumbs and index fingers, tilt their heads back and coil the maple syrup taffy into their mouths. Enjoy.

Of course there were other uses for maple syrup, though my grand-mother used very little as an ingredient in recipes. She served it on pancakes, crepes and as a dip for buttered, fresh-baked bread.

That the way we do it in those days

There were really only two men in my grandmother's life: the one she thought she wanted to marry and the one she married.

She met the first man one summer Sunday afternoon.

In the early years of the 1900s, rural prairie settlers often gathered for house parties or at dances at the local schoolhouse on Friday or Saturday nights after their evening chores. The Fradettes, part of the close-knit French-Canadian community, also liked to get together with their kinsmen on Sundays after Mass. My grandmother and Audelie looked forward to Sundays because, under their father's strict rule, they rarely were allowed to go to the other weekend social events. She recalled this with a clear tone of disgust.

"My dad, he don't want us going no place that he can't watch us. If he don't go, we don't go either." Her voice rose a little. "And *Mon Dieu*, we have so many chores every day we don't get to go no place anyhow. But after Mass, well, everybody get together then. He can't say no on Sundays."

When she recalled those afternoon gatherings her voice changed, held a note of giddy enthusiasm.

"Yes, they were very good parties. The mens push everything to the walls in the living room, and sometime they even take the furniture and put it outside … but that was only in the summer … so everybody can dance."

She would look up, her eyes sideways to the ceiling as if she could see the scene clearly there.

"Somebody play the fiddle, somebody else play the mouth organ. Sometime people, they get up and sing ... your Auntie Audelie and me, we used to sing duets ... and the mens, they pass around a jug of homebrew. Oh, some of those guys, they get pretty drunk but, you know, everybody work hard in those days, so they let off some steam ... it was nothing," she'd say, shrugging her shoulders, her lips puckering in a soft kiss-like O.

The hostess of the party always provided plenty of food – stacks of sandwiches and pickles, and lots of baked goods. Children got to play with neighbour kids and cousins. Women, isolated on their farms all week, were happy to visit one another, exchange their complaints and maybe a few recipes, while the men drank and smoked and talked about crops and livestock. Teenagers, priming for marriage, flirted and courted under the watchful eyes of their parents. Many times relatives and friends of local families came to these functions, some having travelled considerable distances, to visit and give their young men and women the opportunity to seek out potential partners. In the midst of all of this, of course, everyone danced.

One Sunday afternoon my grandmother, then fifteen years old, met a young man visiting from Deleau, Manitoba, a good day's buggy ride east of her home. When my sisters and I asked her about him years later, out of our own romantic curiosities, we all remember the same voice, small and reflective, soft and certain and, above all, secretive.

"Yes, he was such a nice man. He treat me very good."

She shared few details of their meeting, but from what she told me about these family parties and what I know of her life then, I think that on that afternoon their eyes caught in a moment of laughter, he sitting a few people away from her, as they watched someone stomp an enthusiastic jig, that she flushed and looked away, her heart thumping in a manner unfamiliar to her, and that three or maybe four songs later this man of small stature, self-assured with kind eyes, managed to corner her beside the refreshment table. And I think it would have been the sound of his voice – gentle and smooth – that drew her to him.

"Well, of course, he had to go back home to Deleau. It was summer. Everybody have lots to do on the farm at that time of year. So we write letters back and forth," she told us. "Yes ... he write me some nice things in those letters."

My grandmother never spoke of the details but his words must have been tender and attentive, smoothing away the roughness of her father's gruff manner, her brothers' nonchalance.

"We write each other until he go to the war. Then I find out from some people who know his family, he get kill over there. Oh, I cry when I get that news." She looked down at her hands folded in her lap and shook her head. "Nobody know why I cry so much. I think maybe … maybe I marry that guy, you know? But … well …"

My mother tells me that for a long time my grandmother kept a small photograph of this young man, along with a few other treasured items, in one of her storage trunks. I seem to remember that once she showed me that picture. It was a three by five, black-and-white photograph, its white edges frayed and turning grey-brown. In it his head is turned a little to the left, his shoulders squared slightly to the right. His hair, light in colour and smoothed back, lies close to his scalp and forms two arcs on his forehead, a hint of the baldness that would have come in his old age had he lived. Thin lips, almost turned into a smile, seem unusual for the stoic portraits typical of that era. I see the smooth pad of my grandmother's thumb absently rubbing the edge of the photo as she tells bits and pieces of their first meeting and about the letters he wrote to her. And I hear her say, "From the first time I meet him I know he's a kind man. I see it in his eyes, that kindness." I think I have known such eyes: clear, the pupils not too small or too big, direct but not piercing, open wide yet hinting at the squeeze of laughter at their outside edges.

But the photograph disappeared, along with his letters – everything left only to my grandmother's memory and maybe the occasional dream, where she danced the minuet in the arms of her first love, her head tilted back, a knowing smile on her face, his lips pressed to her ear, whispering.

Several years later, Isaie Lacaille and his brother, Henri, arrived by horse and buggy from their family's homestead in Ogema, some forty miles northwest of Radville, to visit and with the likely purpose of inspecting the local French families for potential brides. The Laboissiers, mutual friends of the Lacailles and the Fradettes, gave a party at their home in their honour, and in a rare congenial moment, Ferdinand gave his consent for the girls to attend the gathering chaperoned by their older brother Adélard.

The room would have been filled with the buzz of chatter and loud guffaws of laughter, encouraged by swigs of homebrew and sweet, red wine. Marie-Anne and Audelie had just taken a turn singing a duet for the crowd. My grandmother blushed, shy in spite of her performance, and moved out of the spotlight into the throng of people, while Audelie floated to the edge of the room to talk to Henri, their heads leaning into one another, though their bodies kept a respectable distance.

"Oh, from that first time they meet, my sister have eyes for Henri," my grandmother recalled, "and your grampa, he make eyes with me a little bit that night, too."

She watched Isaie step up to the musicians. He spoke in a low voice as they tinkled and retuned their instruments, then pulled a mouth organ from his pants pocket, and in the next moment the room was alive with music. The guitar strummed, sweet, solid sounds of the violin rose, and Isaie, his hands cupped over the wood and silver, splayed his fingers with the beat, sending out waves of whines and rolls that brought people to their feet, heads bobbing in a happy jig. He stomped his foot and rocked his body to his own music, eyes roaming the crowd in satisfaction.

"Yes, he start looking over at me while he play ... and I think maybe he come to talk to me. And sure enough, he did."

But she was not as taken with him as Audelie was with his brother, despite his good looks – his angular face, blue-green eyes and full-lipped smile. That night they spoke only a few words. I imagine the conversation went something like this:

"You're a Fradette girl, eh?"

"*Oui, je suis.* My people came from Saint-Lazare de Bellechasse. In Quebec. And you?"

"Notre-Dame-de-Lourdes, Manitoba, since the 1880s. Before that, who knows!"

"They like each other, those two. Henri and Audelie."

"Yes, I think so. You play good on the mouth organ."

"*Merci.* I play the violin too ... Will you dance with me?"

"*Oui, merci.*"

And from this brief meeting the two began an unlikely, formal courtship.

"Audelie and Henri, they write letters back and forth," my grandmother told me, "and she say every time that Isaie, he ask about me."

I can almost hear the enthusiastic innocence in Audelie's voice, "Oh, look, Henri say that Isaie, he send his regards. He want to write to you. I think he like you, Marie-Anne. *Oui,* he does, I'm sure."

My grandmother recalled, "You know, he was very handsome, your grampa ... always smiling ... a very, very good dancer, too." She considered good humour and the ability to dance important quali-ties in a man. But unlike Audelie's response to Henri's letters, she didn't swoon over those my grandfather sent her from British Columbia, where he had gone to work in the mines maybe hoping – as many young men of that time did – to make his fortune. I wonder if her feelings for the man from Deleau still lingered, or maybe she was afraid to give herself over to the dream of a new life, fearing that something would happen to ruin it. But as time passed, it seems that Audelie's exuberance about the future drew my grandmother into the dream, or it is possible that her sister wore her down.

"We'll finally be out of this place, Marie-Anne. No more cows. No more chores. Henri say the Lacaille women don't do work like we do. He say Lacaille women, they get treated with respect. Henri, he want to marry me. Isaie, he want to marry you. Maybe we get married together, eh? Get away from here? We both be Madame Lacaille. What about that, eh?"

Well aware of my grandmother's stubborn streak, Audelie must have gone on and on in long monologues like this – while they were alone milking cows, in whispers as they churned butter, in a hushed chatter by the light of the moon through the window as they lay side by side in bed – making a case for the Lacaille brothers' proposals of marriage that would give them their long-desired emancipation.

"Yes, dear," she told me, "so I marry your grampa. I don't know him very well but he seem like a good man ..." she shrugged her shoulders, "well, that the way we do it in those days ..."

At eighteen and twenty, she and Audelie were certainly of marry-ing age; their father finally gave his blessing and let them go.

On February 22, 1921, Henri and Audelie and Isaie and Marie-Anne wed in a double ceremony in the Catholic church in Radville. The photographs taken that day show Mr. and Mrs. Henri Lacaille serene, mouths almost upturned to smiles; Mr. and Mrs. Isaie Lacaille, wide-eyed, appear tentative, maybe hopeful, or possibly afraid. Both couples took up residence near Ogema with the rest of the Lacaille family, and their presence, formally announced in the local newspaper:

On Tuesday March the 29th, Messrs. Henry and Isaac Lachille
gave a very pleasant party to their friends and neighbors, to
give all an opportunity of meeting their brides. The grooms
received the guests, and the brides looked most charming
with circlets of orange blossoms in their hair and wearing
dainty suits with white crepe over blouses. Mr. H. Reid of
Ogema, was master of ceremonies. Introductions over the
neighbors passed in a circle, by the two happy couples,
wishing them every joy. Following this a jolly few hours were
spent, when the luncheon was served by the mother of the
bridegrooms. All enjoyed the bountiful spread and after a
few dances the evening was concluded. The brides each
received a silver pyrex pie plate as a slight token of good
wishes from their near neighbors present during the evening.

Though the two sisters had married brothers, their new husbands
were distinctly different. Henri Lacaille, forward-thinking and ambi-
tious, had his own homestead not far from his parents' farm near
Ogema. He and Audelie settled on his land, which he worked
successfully for nine years before moving to live south of Radville,
near the Fradette clan. There, Henri bought land, expanded his
farming operation and served as a land councillor in Division Three
for twelve years. During that time, Audelie bore four children and
cared for them, Henri and their home. And, true to her husband's
word, she never milked another cow in the sixty-one years they were
married.

But Isaie and Marie-Anne's life took quite a different turn. My
grandfather had never made a land claim, and the job in the mines
of British Columbia proved fortuneless. Due to a workers' strike, he
returned to Ogema after only a few months with little money and no
direction for his future. I'm not sure how he thought he would
provide for his new wife after they married, and now I wonder if he
thought of it at all. With no home and no job, the couple ended up
moving in with Isaie's parents, Louis and Soufrine.

"Oh, I was so lonely living in that house," my grandmother put
her hands to her face and clicked her tongue, the tisk thick like the
emotion in her voice. "That Soufrine, she never like me being in her
house."

The Lacailles, though French, were a different sort, their history
more convoluted than the Fradettes' direct line of generations of
Quebec farmers. Soufrine was born the daughter of a bricklayer and

lived in Massachusetts before her family immigrated to southern Manitoba. And Louis, born in Montreal and educated as a lawyer, gave up city life and his profession to homestead a piece of uninhabited land near Notre-Dame-de-Lourdes. He seemed to be a loner and not at all interested in building a dynasty like Ferdinand Fradette; a quiet rebel shunning the expected norms of the time.

"He was a different kind of guy ... sort of a hippie," my mother tells me. "These days, that's what people would say he was."

It is unclear as to why Louis and Soufrine moved from Manitoba to Ogema, Saskatchewan, with their seven children. It seems that they only exchanged one set of homesteading hardships for another. The landscapes of the two provinces were very similar in the southern parts back then – miles of flat, raw land with an occasional small roll of hills dipping toward a serpentine river, and everything thick with grasses and brush, many sections rife with stones. The job of clearing the land took every hand, every family member's dedicated work. In this, the Lacailles' and the Fradettes' were the same, and Marie-Anne, who understood the work of maintaining a farm, was willing to do her part in its care. But in the Lacaille household, Isaie's mother had the final say and she categorically rejected my grandmother.

"She think I'm stupid because I don't know how to cook. But she don't teach me. She don't let me do nothing. She never say a nice thing to me." My grandmother would sigh in frustration at these remembrances. "I want to learn, but she won't let me help. Sometime she don't even let me in the kitchen. She shoo me out the door like a dog. Louis, he try to be good to me ... but that ol' lady, she rule the roost."

I can hear Soufrine's accusation ring out, *"Mon Dieu!* You don't know how to cook?"

And, my grandmother stands, eyes to the floor, hands clutched and white-knuckled saying, "No, Madame. I milk the cows ... and do the chores in the yard. My older sisters, they helped my mama in the kitchen."

"A woman's work is in the kitchen. Not out there, eh?" she says, nodding like a horse in the direction of the door, her arms crossed tightly across her chest.

"Oui, Madame."

Her mother-in-law – a small, sturdy woman with a thin-lipped, downturned mouth and coal-black hair pulled back tightly in a bun at the back of her neck – was so cantankerous at times that she wouldn't let her sit at the dinner table, leaving my grandmother hungry and shedding silent tears.

"Your grampa, he say, 'oh, that just the way she is.'" She shrugged and puckered as she said this, mimicking the offhand comment. Then, with a deep breath, she sat forward in her chair and put her hands out flat on her thighs, "So, then he say to me, 'you clean the house up nice. That make her happy.' So I clean everything," she said, waving her hand in the air, "real good. Every day. And that woman, she still don't say nothing. She don't even look at me!"

Everything in my grandmother's life had changed. She longed for the familiar and even may have thought of her father without disdain in those first few months of marriage. I think it was probably the only time in her life that she ever wished for a few cows to tend. At least she knew where she stood with them. And after a courtship of only letters, she found getting to know her new husband a delicate ordeal. And nothing surprised her more than to discover, not long after they were first married, that he could neither read nor write.

It would have happened one such evening, perhaps as she washed the supper dishes, while her new husband and mother-in-law sat together at the kitchen table. By the light of a kerosene lamp, Soufrine mended socks with a large silver needle strung with black wool and Isaie had a Country Guide spread open flat in front of him. He turned the page from left to right as if reading it from the back, forward, then leaned in and looked intently at the magazine. My grandmother stopped her work and watched him. Again he turned a page, left to right. She smiled.

"Isaie, why are you reading that backwards?"

He shrugged, not looking up.

"He's not reading," Soufrine said, her face intent upon her task, "He don't know how to read."

Isaie glanced over at his mother, then swept a quick look at his wife and shrugged again. "I never like school."

"But …" she didn't know what to say.

Soufrine stopped darning and threw her a disapproving glare, "It don't matter if he can or he can't." Isaie's mother was also illiterate.

And with that, my grandmother decided to say nothing.

"So," she recalled, "I wonder … how'd he write me all those letters? Then finally he tell me, one of the other mens he work with in the mines write for him … and sometime Henri, he write for him, too. But, you know, he sign his name on that certificate when we get married," she shrugged, "so I don't think nothing about it."

The scrawl of his signature was the only writing my grandfather ever learned.

I have always been curious about what seemed to be the dismissive way the Lacailles handled their son's inability to read or write. Though illiteracy was not uncommon in people of their era, it seemed unusual in this family, considering Louis's extensive education, and because all the other children were well-schooled in both reading and writing. Maybe Soufrine's illiteracy somehow made his acceptable. These days, she or my grandfather might have been diagnosed with learning disabilities. But back then, her illiteracy was of little consequence to the needs of the family and they seemed to be content to think of Isaie as just a jovial fellow with an ear for music when, in fact, he was creatively talented, adept at carpentry, an inventor of gadgets and a skilled musician. However, he was insecure about his illiteracy and tried to hide it over most of his life.

My mother tells me that my grandfather was known for carrying a small pad of paper and a pencil in his shirt pocket, which he pulled out during discussions, especially about finances or farm business. He would look into the air, crinkle his face into a deep frown and then announce his opinion by touching the tip of the pencil to his tongue and writing scribbles on the pad, as if he were listing his thoughts, important and requiring permanent record.

As easygoing as he generally seemed to be, sometimes he could be inordinately stubborn, maybe to assert his authority and demand the respect his own insecurity would not let him lay hold of. This caused my grandmother heartache over the years.

"I don't know ... sometime your grampa, he have such crazy ideas." She shook her head and stared at the floor, as she began to recall one incident. "I save some extra money from selling my butter and eggs, and from those turkeys I raise. I save for a whole year. Then I tell your grampa I want to buy a new chesterfield with the pullout bed. The one we have was so old and lumpy. We need a new one for the winter."

My uncles, Ernie and Edward, who slept up in the attic in the summer, used the sofa bed in the living room during the cold winter months.

"'No!' he say to me just like that, 'I need that money to buy a new tractor,'" she leaned back and folded her arms across her chest. "I don't like that but what do I say? I don't want to get into no fight with him ... and a tractor, it help us plenty in the fields."

The next day he drove into the yard perched on an old, rusted tractor, the size one would use for yard cleanup rather than for pulling machinery.

"He come home grinning like a little kid with that old rattletrap, and I say to him, 'What is this thing?' Well, I don't know if I should laugh or cry."

"Then he say to me, 'this is the new tractor. I got a real good deal.'" And when my grandmother told me this I imagined my grandfather grinning wide, his eyes glinting like they always did when he was excited.

The next morning he sauntered out to the yard and hooked the tiller to the back of the new tractor. He revved its rattling engine. When he put it in gear nothing moved except the tractor's front end, which reared up like a stallion and then plunked to the ground with a quiet thud. He sat there for some time, the engine chugging and whining, then turned it off, unhooked the tiller and went to fetch the team of horses instead.

"You know, we never talk about that damn tractor again ... well, it take me a whole year to save up some more money for that new chesterfield and I don't let him have a penny, no matter what he say." With this, my grandmother laughed.

They lived with Isaie's parents for six months. Unlike the Fradette men, or even his brother Henri, Isaie showed little desire or ambition for farming. I wonder now if my grandfather's reluctance to take on the responsibilities of a farm was a result of his insecurities. Maybe his happy-go-lucky, lackadaisical attitude was really a mask for his fears, but because of it my grandmother began to feel responsible for their future and started to assert herself.

"I want to leave so bad," she recalled, "oh, what I would do to get out of that house."

It is as if I could hear her whisper her plea to him every night in their tiny room – "Isaie, can we leave here, *s'il te plaît?* We can find a place of our own ... we work together, you and me, side by side. I help you farm. I promise ..." – until he finally found a small piece of land to rent. The house was no more than a shack, only one room with a rusty old stove and buckling wood floor. From the outside it tilted distinctly to the right. But my grandmother didn't care. She was just glad to be out of the elder Lacailles' home and into one she could make her own. And she kept her promise to her husband and worked side by side with him on the little piece of rented land near Ogema.

A year after they had been on their own, Ferdinand made overtures towards them about returning to Radville, saying he would help them buy their own piece of land. I am told that my great-grandfather was the kind of man who wanted all his children around him to watch over them and to solidify his family's place in the community. Though my grandmother wanted to live far away from the memories of her childhood, I think she hoped that maybe her father's offer meant he would finally give her the care and protection she had always longed for from him.

"I was so lonely in that ol' shack. And, you know ... I miss my mama, too. So we decide, yes, we go back to Radville."

And so it was settled. In 1923, the second year of their marriage, my grandparents moved back to that place she thought she hated but decided to love because, at least, it was familiar. They rented a farm only a few miles up the road from her childhood home, and eventually purchased it on their own – Ferdinand's offer to help never materialized.

Grand-père et Grand-mère

When my grandmother left her mother-in-law's home for her own all those many years ago, she took with her a couple of Soufrine's recipes: grand-père et grand-mère (a stew with dumplings) and chocolate pie. Tranche may have been one of them, too, but she would never give Soufrine credit for it. As far as my grandmother was concerned, she learned to make tranche from her own mother; and she'd say of Soufrine, "I never learn a damn thing from that woman," and then add defiantly, "she didn't cook very good, anyway."

I know my grandmother carried disquieting memories of those first tender months of her marriage, but I can see how that time of her life shaped her and that, in fact, she did learn from "that woman" – maybe out of necessity, but she learned – so that when she finally had her own small kitchen in that first rented shack, she was well-prepared to be the matron of her home. She made Soufrine's recipes often because they were my grandfather's favourites. Both are sparse, reflective of those early years of the twentieth century and also of the basic, no-fuss woman they came from.

I asked my mother how the stew and dumplings got its name, and she said, "I don't really know. That's just what we always called it, I suppose because it was Grandma Lacaille's recipe." Then after thinking for awhile she added, "My dad was the one who called it 'grand-père et grand-mère.' Sometimes he made up funny names for things. He was like that, you know."

As my great-grandmother and grandmother did for their families, my mother also made this rib-sticking stew for us, usually on cold winter evenings on the same day that she baked bread so that sopping the gravy was even more delightful. These days, I serve it in a bowl over mashed potatoes, topped with lightly steamed broccoli crowns and replace the bread with a spoon to slurp the gravy.

Measurements and quantities in meat dishes are fairly flexible, as a little less water or a bit more flour has no great effect upon the end product. But baking demands exact measurements, which makes my grandmother's ability in the kitchen so much more astonishing to me. But hers must have been perfect, in her own look-see-feel kind of way, because by the time my mother remembers being the recipient of her culinary gifts everything always tasted perfectly delicious. This was not the case when I attempted to make Soufrine's chocolate pie, though the recipe my mother recited to me in that alcove of my family room is the one she observed my grandmother make and also used herself with great success over the years.

I confess here and now that I am impatient with precise measurements, thus baking is not my strong suit. However this recipe seemed simple – a cup of sugar, some cocoa, cornstarch and water. Easy. So one evening I decided to make it for my dinner guests. I had a basil-chicken-sausage lasagna in the oven and had sliced some zucchinis, onions, red peppers and mushrooms in preparation for a sauté. The green salad with cherry tomatoes and Gorgonzola sprinkles chilled in the refrigerator, ready for dressing. I expected my guests to arrive in about twenty minutes, so I had just enough time to whip up the chocolate pie filling. My mouth watered as I remembered my grandmother serving it – the taste of its smooth richness, nestled in a buttery pie crust and topped with fresh whipped cream. I was excited to announce this dessert to my guests as an old family recipe.

According to the recipe's instructions I put the dry ingredients in a pot on the stove, added a cup of boiling water, turned up the heat and began stirring, making sure to pay close attention to the mixture because it is supposed to thicken fast. I stirred, and stirred, and stirred some more. I looked at the clock and thought, I should time this stirring process so I can add that to the recipe. Five minutes already may have passed. I stood, left hand on my hip, stirred with my right, and watched the clock … ten more minutes went by and I began to think about that small notation at the beginning of the recipe, which says: *It thickens fast!* I wondered if what that meant to my grandmother seventy-five years ago could have even slightly the same meaning to me. Me, part of the instant generation – Jell-O pudding in five minutes, long grain rice in ten; fast food, fast cash, instant coffee, instant messaging – and as my mind ran through all the "instants" that my grandmother never had, I also realized that I was running out of time; my guests could be at the door in … in an instant! Still stirring, I picked up the portable phone, which is never far from my reach, and punched in my mother's number.

"Mom!"

"Oh hi, honey. What a nice surprise."

"Mom! I'd love to chat but I'm making chocolate pie and my dinner guests are almost here and the stuff's not thickening."

"How much cornstarch did you use?"

For good measure, I rattled off the list of ingredients and exactly what I'd done so far.

"Oh well, you've got to add more cornstarch."

"How much?" My voice was rather high-pitched and a bit squeaky at this point.

"As much as you need until it thickens. But watch out, it'll thicken fast."

I rolled my eyes. What I would have given to have my grandmother at my side just then, to whip that chocolate filling into the silky-smooth pudding she always made without effort, her eyes crinkling in amusement at my ineptness. Instead I hung up the phone and mixed some cornstarch and a few tablespoons of water. Then I stirred it into my yet-watery concoction and pleaded "*Mon Dieu*" under my breath hoping the French god of cooking would rescue this catastrophe.

The doorbell rang.

"Somebody get that, please! I can't leave the stove."

In the midst of welcomes and greetings, my chocolate pie filling finally thickened, in a manner of speaking. I poured it into the pie shell and then excused myself for a moment to change my shirt, which was unusually moist with perspiration. Later, I offered blueberries with whipped cream as an alternative to the chocolate pie and kept quiet about the "old family recipe."

The next day I called my mother to report on my shaky success. "It thickened, but it didn't taste like the chocolate pie I remember Gramma making. Are you sure she used water and not milk?"

"Yes, I'm sure."

"Why wouldn't she use milk? She always had milk on the farm. It would thicken easier if you used milk."

"Well, that was Dad's mom's recipe. He liked it, so that's how Mom made it. And let's put it this way, Soufrine didn't have much imagination when it came to cooking."

"Mmm … yeah, I remember Gramma saying something like that."

I tried the recipe again, this time not for guests, but I was still dissatisfied with the result, so more telephone conversations with my mother ensued.

"Mom, it's still not thickening right."

"Well, I called Helen." My Aunt Helen, my mother's youngest sister, lives in Red Deer, Alberta, and has given us a great deal of help with my grandmother's recipes. "She says it's the cornstarch."

"What do you mean the cornstarch? I'm still not using enough?"

"No, she says the cornstarch is different in the States. She says she always used to take her own cornstarch with her when she went down south." Down south means here in Arizona where, like my parents, my aunt and uncle came to spend the winter months away from the Canadian cold.

"How can that be?"

"That's what she says. The consistency is way different."

"Hmm … maybe organic cornstarch will work," I offered.

"Organic?" my mother laughed. "Maybe you just need new cornstarch … how old's that stuff you have in your cupboard … five years … ten years old?"

"Geez, I don't know … could be. I don't use it much when I cook," I confessed. "Yeah, I'll get new cornstarch … organic, if I can find such a thing … and try it again."

This chocolate pie recipe, well, as my grandmother often said about many things in life, "Sooner or later I'll get it right."

GRAND-PÈRE ET GRAND-MÈRE

Stew:

2 tablespoons of butter
1 pound cubed stewing meat
1 medium cooking onion, sliced
Salt and pepper, to taste
2 cups (approximately) of water
4-6 more cups of water including potato water

Heat butter in a big iron pot until it begins to bubble. Add meat, and at medium-high heat, turn and stir pieces to brown on all sides. Add onion, salt and pepper. Cook for five minutes. Add 2 cups of water or more if needed to cover meat and reduce heat to medium-low, cover and cook for 2 – 3 hours, slowly adding about 4 more cups of water during that time. If serving with boiled potatoes, add the potato water to the pot to enhance flavour of the stew. When meat is cooked and tender, add dumplings.

Dumplings:

1 cup flour
2 teaspoons baking powder
1/2 cup of milk (approximately)

Mix flour and baking powder, then add enough milk to make a soft dough. On a well-floured surface, use a rolling pin to spread dough to 1/4 inch thickness. Cut dough into 1 1/2 inch squares. The dough will be sticky so use lots of flour to pick up each piece and drop into the stew pot. The extra flour helps to thicken the juice into a nice gravy. Simmer for 1/2 hour. Serve with boiled potatoes and lots of bread to sop up the gravy.

Note: the dumplings don't rise, but rather have the look and texture of thick squares of pasta.

CHOCOLATE PIE
It thickens fast!

1 cup white sugar
1 tablespoon cocoa
3 tablespoons cornstarch
3/4 cup boiling water
A small piece of butter
1 regular pie shell, baked

Combine dry ingredients in a cooking pot on the stove and turn heat to medium. Add boiling water, stir constantly until mixture thickens. Add butter, stir until melted and pour into pie shell. Leave on kitchen counter to cool and then refrigerate until ready to serve. Top with heavy whipped cream.

In my *many* attempts to get this recipe right, I have discovered that when I leave the dry ingredients on the heated stove for a few minutes so the sugar just barely begins to melt and then add the boiling water, most often it actually does thicken quite quickly and is much closer in texture to the beautifully smooth pudding my grandmother made. It could be that this is actually one of the steps in the recipe – but an unconscious one. One that happened naturally for my grandmother who was always in the midst of many tasks to single-handedly prepare meals for her family of seven.

I can see it so clearly – nearing the end of her dinner preparations, my grandmother starts the kettle to boil the water and quickly puts the sugar, cocoa and cornstarch in a pot on the hot stove. She moves to the counter to slice a loaf of bread and then back to the stove to poke the boiling potatoes, which are done. She drains off the potato water into the roasting pan where the juice from the roast waits to be made into gravy. As she stirs the lovely brown juice, the kettle whistles; she pours the cup of water – only measured by sight, of course – into the now warmed dry mixture for the pie and stirs. Voila!

Everybody just try to survive

My grandmother was pregnant with her first child, my mother, Florence, when she and my grandfather moved back to Radville. There, over the course of the next twenty years, they had four more children – Ernest, Edward, Eva and Helen – and together lived through some of the most difficult conditions on record in North American history: the dirty thirties, a decade of unprecedented drought and economic depression. While hundreds of farmers across the Canadian prairies and the Midwest of the United States gave up their homesteads due to exhaustion and starvation, my grandparents managed to survive. Somehow they held on during those hot, cloudless days of summer drought, the wind howling through tiny cracks around the window frames of their two-room house. My grandmother stuffed old rags in the gaps she could see but, still, a blanket of fine dust lined the sills, powdered the furniture and made the wood floor grind with every step. Day after day they watched dirt blow into dunes against the yard fence and prayed for the rain that would not come – tumbleweeds rolling in the field; listless cows foraging for prickly Russian thistles or snippets of sunburned grass; chickens pecking the ground baked into stone, their brown feathers ruffling in the wind.

Sometimes eerie spokes of lightning filled the sky and seemed to promise rain but instead only fuelled prairie fires that coloured the horizon with jagged rays of brilliant orange, the terrifying imposters of a setting sun. Together the family huddled in the doorway, watchful but helpless should the fire eat its way in their direction. Helpless,

too, when the army worms marched up the road in a black blanket
that eventually covered their home, the frail prairie foliage and the
trees. And after they passed, every sign of plant life was gone and the
land, bared even further to the perils of wind. Other times locusts
came in agitating, billowing clouds, leaving the same carnage
behind. While the heavens and the earth remained barren, other
parts of it flourished. Along with the insects, rabbits multiplied by
the thousands. It is hard to comprehend how nature could turn on
itself as profoundly as it did.

"They used to have rabbit drives," my grandmother recalled.
"Everybody, the mens, us women, even the kids went. We hold hands
and shoo those rabbits into one place, sort of a pen, and then the
mens use big clubs to kill them … it was just terrible." She shrugged
her shoulders, "But what could you do? Those damn things, they eat
everything! The land, the little bit of garden we try to grow … everything bare to the dirt. You know, everybody just try to survive back
then."

My grandparents did survive through hard work, a good dose of
stubbornness and the support of their community. Everyone knew
everyone: the Fradette brothers' and Henri and Audelie Lacaille's
farms to the south; the Hurlburt's, Larsen's and Rasmussen's farms to
the north, the latter being neighbours who had become friends. They
credited one another for staying put while many packed up what
little they had left and moved to towns to find work or to northwest-
ern Alberta where the drought had been more forgiving and land was
still available to farm. They supported one another with words of
encouragement in the dust of summer and kept company together in
the long months of winter, sharing meals – no matter how sparse –
and evenings of card games and conversation next to the warmth of a
coal stove.

My grandfather particularly enjoyed the company of these
friends, as the men seemed less competitive than their French relatives, whom he may have felt judged him for his lack of farming
ambition. My grandmother enjoyed them, too. If she felt like a family
outcast because of her husband, with their friends she was at least
free from criticism, probably admired for her industry and could be
part of a larger world, one in which she spoke English rather than
French and learned the ways of others, some of whom had immigrated from Denmark and England; others from Minnesota and
South Dakota.

But despite the tensions and unspoken defenses that swirled about her family, my grandmother's need for them, especially her mother, was etched deep in her being. My mother recalls, as a small child, going on many visits to the elder Fradettes' home, just a few miles down the road from their farm.

"Sometimes when Henri, Mom's brother, was in from doing his chores, he'd play hide and seek with me ... I'd hide under the staircase that went up to the bedrooms. He'd sit there on the stairs and wait for me to come out ... funny what you remember as a child."

Other times she just sat with my grandmother in Philomène's kitchen, sipping a glass of milk while the two women talked quietly in French; the kitchen that once held a boisterous family of seven boys and four girls, a great and constant flurry of activity and noise, comings and goings, and endless cooking. The kitchen where now my great-grandmother would sit, in a rocking chair, the click of needles knitting grandchildren's mittens, a can of Copenhagen snuff bulging from her apron pocket; unhurried now, with only Ferdinand, herself and the two youngest boys, Emile and Henri, to cook for. Except, of course, on special occasions, like Christmas Eve after midnight Mass, when everyone – sons and daughters, spouses and children – would gather for a meal, music and homebrew; occasions when it seemed everyone let go of their judgments and celebrated the year's bounty, however big or small.

Some of the family didn't know what to make of my grandmother. My mother remembers a few comments among the Fradette wives. "Why is she making all that work for herself?" they'd say. French women didn't do what she did, even in the worst of times. Traditionally, on the farm, they were expected to be good wives, which meant waiting on their husbands, caring for the children, sometimes ten or more, and tending to homemaking duties – cooking, cleaning and gardening. Few took on producing butter and cream as an industry. Some traded eggs for store credit but few turned it into the weekly business my grandmother made of it. They started tisking a little when she took up raising turkeys to butcher and sell in the late fall, though many of them reserved one or two from her flock because they knew she would grow them lovely and fat, and perfect for Christmas dinner. And they simply could not understand why she would work like a hired man in the field stooking wheat and pitching hay.

She may have been trying to make up for the drive and enterprise my grandfather lacked, or maybe she was being stubbornly loyal to the promise she made him in those first months of marriage. But I think, beyond this, she was, and always had been, a woman of her own means and desires, and I marvel at how those years of drought and depression, in fact, ignited her verve and creativity.

Like most farmers in southern Saskatchewan during the thirties, she and her family lived on relief sent from other provinces: root vegetables – potatoes, turnips and carrots – a portion of dried salt cod, and the occasional wheel of yellow cheese and box of apples. But they also tried to maintain some livestock for meat, eggs, milk and butter. If they could afford to buy a hog, it ate kitchen scraps and leftover milk from the separating process, and the chickens were fed grain salvaged from the ravages of the heat and insects. The federal government issued monthly food stamps for staple supplies such as flour, sugar and coffee, and my grandmother traded her dairy and eggs for the rest.

"Yes, well … you know I take maybe sixteen, seventeen pounds of my butter and a crate of eggs to Radville every week and then they give me credit at the store. That's how I buy things like honey and peanut butter, cocoa and baking powder, things I need to cook with … yes, and I always get some fruit … maybe some peaches … and in the winter I get those nice, little, Christmas oranges … and some bologna for the kids' sandwiches," my grandmother recalled.

Andrea, one of my grandmother's nieces, remembers, too, "Sometimes I stayed overnight at their house during the week. Your mum and I, we were like sisters, so we did that quite often. And I liked staying there because *Ma Tante* always made the best lunches for school … a nice sandwich … you know, most of us kids just had two pieces of bread with lard in it, but *Ma Tante* always put meat in hers … and there was always a piece of fruit in that lunch box."

I love the way Andrea says, *"Ma Tante,"* the two words flowing together as one, the pronunciation deeply French. She's now over eighty years old, but still speaks of her aunt, her godmother, with glowing admiration.

"She kept such a nice house … doilies everywhere."

"Do you think my grandmother was a happy woman?" I ask her.

"Well …" We are speaking by telephone; she is silent for a moment. "She was always so busy … she was a little bit crabby sometimes, I have to say … oh no, don't say I said that … I think maybe she had to get mad to get what she wanted around *Oncle Isaie*," she laughs, and I laugh with her. "You laugh just like your mother," she says to me.

I'm sure I've said those same words to my mother.

I think about my grandmother in those years, standing in her kitchen, hands on her hips, wondering what she could possibly feed her family with so few supplies, but then somehow finding a way to craft a dish out of flour, or potatoes, or eggs. When I look at the recipes my mother and I have collected, I can pick out what she created during that time, like a food diary of the Depression. Sometimes, my mother tells me, they only had bread with gravy made from milk, or pie crust filled with mashed potatoes. She used what she had: omelettes in the summer when eggs were more abundant and pancakes in the winter when they were not.

There are times when I think I have inherited my grandmother's creativity in the kitchen. I am told I can cook something out of nothing, make a gourmet meal out of leftovers and, like her, I rarely use a recipe. I go by sight, taste and feel. But I've never had to cook out of that kind of necessity, only out of my own satisfaction at being able to adeptly combine a few lonely items from the refrigerator rather than throw them out. I know how to make; she was forced to make do.

My mother tells me that during the worst years of the Depression, when they were so poor that other provinces were sending farmers in the region clothing donations as well as food, my grandmother would wash these clothes, then tear them apart and use the material to sew new items for her family – dresses, pants and coats. And she used old flour sacks to make bloomers for the girls, and sheets and pillowcases for the beds, and saved all the scraps of leftover fabric from everything she made to braid rugs for the cold wood floors. Long after everyone else had gone to sleep, she sewed by coal-oil lamp using the foot-pump Singer machine she bought "on time" from the Eaton's catalogue.

"I can't afford to pay cash for that machine, so your grampa he say, 'write them a letter and tell them that if they send it to us, we promise to pay five dollars every month 'til it all paid for.' And by gosh, they did. They send it to us … oh, that sewing machine, it help me a lot. I sew all our clothes in those days, you know."

I think about this: my mother wore underwear with the Robin Hood emblem on her behind and a dress made from two old cotton shirts donated by some giving soul from Alberta, but every day she went to school with a fresh piece of fruit in her lunch box.

"Yes, we have some tough years on the farm, but," my grandmother shrugged her shoulders and puckered her lips, "you know, we survive."

Two ways to make a rug

BRAIDING:

Collect old clothing too worn to repair and fabric scraps from sewing. Cut cloth into one- to two-inch wide strips.

Gather three strips of approximately the same length, sew them together at one end and then braid them. After making several lengths of braid, sew those together end-to-end, using very heavy thread, to make one long braid.

Next, begin coiling the long braid, sewing it in a circle or oblong shape and adding more braided pieces until the rug is coiled to the size desired.

You can make rugs as large as three feet wide and four feet long quite easily this way.

WEAVING:

Use an iron wheel from a horse buggy as a frame. Lay it on the kitchen table to make weaving easier.

Cut old clothes and fabric into one- or two-inch wide strips. Sew strips end-to-end until they are long enough to cross the diameter of the wheel's circle and then tie four pieces securely across the iron frame to make eight equal sections.

Starting at the centre of the circle where the strips intersect, weave another strip of cloth over and under the secured pieces. Make only a single circle so that you stop at the same place you began the weave. This is considered one round of weaving.

Now loop new strips of cloth through that first round between each V of fabric and tie the ends to the iron frame.

Make a second round, weaving over and under each strip, as done the first time.

Loop new strips of cloth through the second round between each V and secure those to the frame.

You will need to keep adding to the strip used for the rounds by sewing more pieces end-to-end.

Continue to weave one round of the circle and then add strips between the Vs until a final round is woven at the inside edge of the wheel.

Sew the last round with heavy thread to secure it to all the strips, which are still tied to the frame. This will hold the entire weave in place.

Untie the strip ends from the frame and trim fringe with scissors to make even.

My grandmother spent many long hours in the gloomy days of winter making colourful and beautifully patterned rugs, which she saved until Easter when she did a thorough spring cleaning of the house, often painted or papered the walls, and once nailed down a gently used piece of linoleum in the kitchen all on her own. She used the best of the old rugs to cover the floor of the attic where my mother and uncles slept during the summer months. The rest got relegated to the shanty at the entrance to the house and the yard sheds to use for wiping dirty boots, until they simply fell apart.

Sucre à Crème

CHOCOLATE SOUP

4 cups of milk
1/4 cup sugar (or more, to taste)
1 heaping tablespoon of cocoa
4 (approximately) slices of bread, cubed

Mix the milk, sugar and cocoa in a pot and warm at medium heat until the sugar dissolves. Add bread cubes and serve in soup bowls.

Many winter mornings during the Depression, my grandmother served chocolate soup for breakfast, the milk fresh from the cow and the bread, homemade, before my grandfather took the kids to school by horse and sleigh, huddled under cow skins with hot stones, warmed on the kitchen stove, next to their feet.

MILK GRAVY

3 tablespoons butter
1 medium onion, chopped
2 tablespoons flour

2 cups milk
Salt and pepper, to taste

Melt butter in a saucepan, add the onion and stir until fragrant. Add the flour and stir to make a thick roux; then slowly add the milk, stirring briskly with a fork or whisk to avoid lumps. Continue to stir until the mixture thickens. Add salt and pepper to taste.

Today we would describe this dish as a white sauce, but my grandmother called it milk gravy, maybe because gravy sounded more substantial. She served it over potatoes, along with lots of bread and butter. When times were good and the garden flourishing, she'd use the gravy (with only a bit of onion for flavour) as the "white sauce" for creamed peas, baby onions or cauliflower.

OMELETTE

4 eggs
1 cup milk
3/4 cup flour
Salt and pepper, to taste
1/4 cup melted butter or roast drippings

Preheat oven to 450 degrees. Beat eggs, gradually adding milk, flour, salt and pepper. Continue to beat for a minute or two. Pour butter or drippings into a cast iron fry pan or 12 muffin tins to just cover the bottom of each tin. Pour batter into the pan or equally into tins and bake approximately 15 minutes until the batter puffs up about 3 inches and the top becomes golden brown. Serve immediately.

My grandmother's omelette is not what one would expect traditionally from a French cook, but she called this Yorkshire pudding-like recipe by the same name simply because it was made mostly of eggs. My mother tells me that it was her favourite dish to serve during the Lenten season and as a meatless meal on Fridays, in observance of their Catholic faith. As with most of her cooking my grandmother liked to use cast iron to make an omelette, preferring her frying pan over muffin tins, but it is light and delicious either way. She served it cut into wedges dotted with pads of fresh butter and … yes … always offered potatoes as an accompaniment.

MASHED POTATO PIE

6 medium sized potatoes
1 small onion, finely chopped
1 heaping tablespoon of butter
Salt and pepper, to taste
1 uncooked double pie crust

Cook potatoes. When tender to the fork, drain and mash well.
Add onion, butter and salt and pepper. Mix thoroughly and
put in pie shell. Cover with second crust, fluting the edges
together and making several decorative cuts in the top to
allow venting. Bake in a preheated 400 degree oven for 30 to
35 minutes, or until golden brown.

Potato pie made the most out of very little, but in better times my
grandmother still served it on meatless Fridays or for supper, the
evening meal, which was generally lighter than the substantial
dinner she served at noon, when everyone already had put in long
hours of chores.

BAKING POWDER BISCUITS

3 cups flour
6 teaspoons baking powder
1/2 teaspoon salt
3 teaspoons sugar
3 level tablespoons shortening
Water

Sift dry ingredients in a bowl. Add shortening and combine
until the mixture is like a fine powder. Add enough water to
make a soft dough. Roll out on a floured surface to
approximately 1/2 inch thickness. Cut rounds with a cookie
cutter. Put on a very lightly greased cookie sheet. Bake in a
preheated 450 degree oven for 10 minutes.

If she was running out of bread, my grandmother used to make
biscuits to eat with dinner. If there were any left over – which, my
mother tells me, wasn't too often – they ate them for dessert spread
with jam.

BEEF STEW

2 tablespoons butter
1 pound stewing beef
1 medium sized onion, sliced
Salt and pepper, to taste
1 to 4 cups water
4 medium sized potatoes, peeled and quartered

6 carrots, cut into one-inch pieces
1 small turnip, diced
4 medium sized onions, quartered

Heat butter in a large cooking pot or Dutch oven until it bubbles. Add beef, onions and salt and pepper; turn heat to high and brown meat on all sides, stirring often. Add approximately 1 cup of water, just to cover meat mixture; then cover and simmer, adding a little water occasionally, until meat is well done (approximately 2 hours or until meat is very tender to the fork).

Add vegetables and 2 or more cups of water to pot; enough liquid to cover the mixture. Cook vegetables at a low boil until tender and soft. Serve with lots of bread for dunking.

I'm certain my grandmother created this stew in response to the availability of root vegetables when there was little else so she could stretch a pound of meat into a substantial meal for a hungry crew of seven. I asked my mother if she thought this recipe was born of the stew-with-dumplings dish my great-grandmother Soufrine used to make, as I thought I could see some similarities in them. And I wondered if I could add the dumplings to this beef stew, too.

"Oh no, no, no. That's something completely different. You don't want to do that," she said with just a little huff in her voice. "This stew, this is just the way Mom used to make it."

And I thought, alright then, I'm not messing with tradition.

OATMEAL COOKIES

1 cup sugar
1 cup lard
2 eggs
1/4 cup milk
1 teaspoon each of cinnamon, cloves and nutmeg
1 1/2 teaspoon vanilla
2 cups oatmeal
2 cups flour
1 teaspoon baking powder
1 cup raisins (if you have them)

Mix all ingredients in above order; blend well and then drop by teaspoons full on to a lightly greased cookie sheet. Bake in a preheated 375 degree oven for 10 to 12 minutes.

I can't remember a time when my grandmother did not have a batch of oatmeal cookies on hand, nor can my mother even in the worst of the thirties. I imagine her back then, doling out the cinnamon, cloves and nutmeg in lesser quantities, the cookies not quite so rich and delightful to the tongue, but by skimping just a little on those precious spices she knew she would have enough to make the next batch. And at the grocery store on Saturday, in those years when supplies were rationed, she would count up her store credit and whisper to Jack Seede, the manager, "You save me my spices. Next week, I buy some."

RAISIN PUDDING

Part one:

1 cup flour
1/2 cup of milk
2 teaspoons baking powder
Pinch of salt
2 tablespoons sugar
1 cup raisins
2 tablespoons butter

Mix all ingredients and pour into an 8 or 9 inch square baking pan.

Part two:

1 cup brown sugar
2 cups boiling water
1 tablespoon butter

Combine ingredients and pour sauce over the mixture in the pan. Bake in a preheated 350 degree oven for approximately 30 minutes.

My mother tells me that somehow my grandmother always seemed to have raisins on hand. They came in a large bag and kept well, so I imagine she bought them as she did her spices – when she could – and rationed them out in her own cooking. When she made a dish with raisins everyone enjoyed their sweet richness.

CREAM PUFFS

1/2 cup butter
1 cup boiling water
1 cup flour
4 eggs, individually beaten
1 cup whipping cream
1 teaspoon sugar
Vanilla, to taste

Put butter in a pot on the stove at medium heat and add boiling water. Add the flour slowly, stirring constantly. Add one beaten egg at a time, stirring constantly and making sure each egg is completely combined in the mixture before adding the next one.

Drop by tablespoonful on to a greased cookie sheet. Bake in a preheated 350 degree oven, watching constantly, until golden brown. Remove and let cool.

Whip cream to soft peaks, adding sugar and vanilla until smooth.

When ready to eat, cut off the tops of the puffs, remove and discard their doughy centres. Fill each with the whipped cream. Replace tops and serve.

My grandmother could afford to make what we might consider to be a decadent dessert because, if she had nothing else, she always had her own dairy products. "It took a lot of time to make them. She had to beat those eggs in one at a time," my mother tells me. "Her arm would be going a hundred miles an hour, but they came out so light and fluffy … no one could make cream puffs like Mom."

SUCRE À CRÈME

1 cup brown sugar
1 cup whipping cream
1/2 teaspoon vanilla

Combine sugar and whipping cream in a saucepan on the stove and bring to a boil. Add vanilla and cook for approximately 1 minute. Serve for dessert with slices of bread for dipping.

"Of everything Gramma cooked, what was your favourite?" I asked my mother, Aunt Helen and Uncle Ernie. Without hesitation each said, "Sucre à Crème!" And Aunt Helen added, "We used to eat it with peanut butter and bread … oh, that was so good."

Christmas and White Candy

My grandmother loved to bake, synchronizing preparations of batter and dough, so while one cake baked in the perfectly stoked oven she prepared another. She moved about the kitchen in quiet meditation, always an apron wrapped about her middle, often a dust mark of white flour somewhere on her face. Saturday morning baking was as important to her as Sunday morning Mass. But in early fall, baking day took on another dimension and a whole set of recipes that she prepared only once a year. She began baking for Christmas.

Even through the hardest years on the farm, my grandmother made sure she had some extra credit from her dairy and egg sales at Jack Seede's store and set aside a little money from the turkey harvest to buy the supplies she needed to do that special baking. And she needed plenty on hand because from Christmas Eve through to the New Year she, as well as most of my French-Canadian relatives, had an ongoing stream of guests coming and going, day through evening, to partake in the holiday cheer. Bundled in hides on horse-drawn sleighs, people went from farm to farm to celebrate the season, visiting for lunch or coffee and Christmas baking, maybe dinner and, often, a night of music, filled with dancing and long pulls on jugs of homebrew.

In early autumn, just after Thanksgiving, my grandmother began her holiday preparations by making dark and white Christmas cakes. Spicy and heavy with dried fruit and nuts, she wrapped them in wax paper and stored them in the cellar to "cure" until mid-December, when the season's festivities began. She was known for these cakes and family members often asked her to make the dark one for weddings.

She baked the wedding cakes in a set of three progressively larger round pans, then stacked and covered them in sugar icing. I smile when I think that she was responsible for all those single female wedding guests tucking pieces of her laced-paper-doily wrapped cake into their purses and later slipping them under their pillows at night so they might dream about the men they were going to marry.

My mother and Aunt Helen say that my grandmother also made a special chocolate cake around holiday time, and they still regard it as if it held some quality of otherworldliness. "She made that chocolate almond cake way before the holidays and stored it in wax paper, just like the Christmas cakes," my mother told me, a certain childlike wonder in the tone of her voice, "I don't know why it kept so well for so long … and the colour, the colour of it seemed almost red … it was so delicious."

"And then there were those little knotted doughnuts she made, too," my aunt sighed. "She'd make up a big batch in late November, maybe early December, and keep them frozen in the granary until Christmas and then just warm them in the oven. Oh, we couldn't wait to sink our teeth into them."

She also reserved lovely date-filled oatmeal cookies for the Christmas season, though no one really knows why. Certainly in terms of her baking abilities, they were no more difficult to prepare than many of the others she made every week of the year. But my grandmother had her ways, her traditions. Maybe she knew that reserving them for the holidays would be one more way to make her family feel special.

In times of scarcity, the holiday season with lots of good food and plenty of sweet treats offered the feeling of abundance. There was rarely enough money for actual Christmas presents but my mother, aunts and uncles looked forward to the special treats they had but once a year – rich chocolate fudge, peanut brittle and a strange but wonderful confection my grandmother called "white candy" made of white sugar, white corn syrup, a bit of water and a few drops of maple flavouring. Cookie-looking morsels, each topped with a walnut half, the consistency somewhere between hard candy and fudge, very sweet, just slightly chewy and impossible to replicate. Only my grandmother could consistently make it perfect.

These confections, peanuts in the shell and "Christmas oranges" rounded out the season's bounty. Christmas oranges were actually small, seedless mandarin oranges, available only in December, that my grandmother bought by the wood crate at the grocery store in town. They came individually wrapped in orange tissue paper, which provided an extra seasonal benefit – as soft toilet paper for the outhouse. After it was used up, the big thick Eaton's Christmas catalogue took its place.

Christmas tradition culminated with attending midnight Mass. If the weather was particularly pleasant, after church the family would gather with the rest of the Fradette clan at my great-grandparents' home for tourtière and Philomène's pork and potato ragout. This was a dish my grandmother never chose to make, and one that my mother said tasted like mush. When they finally arrived back home, in the wee hours of Christmas morning, my mother and her siblings put their stockings out for Santa near the stove, next to a glass of milk and a plate of cookies. After an excited sleep they would find Santa's snack gone and each of their stockings filled with nuts, hard candy and an orange, which would be bulging at the end of the toe.

Only once my mother remembers actually getting a Christmas gift, though each year she and the other kids pored over that fat Eaton's catalogue, dreaming about what Santa might bring them.

"Maybe Mom sold a lot of turkeys that year and had some extra money," my mother pondered. "I don't really know. But they did everything to make things nice for us that Christmas."

After scooting the children off to bed, my grandfather clomped around the outside of the house with a lantern and sleigh bells, ho-ho-ho-ing heartily while my grandmother whispered to the kids that they better not get up to look or Santa might not come.

"We knew too darned well that it was Dad out there, but it felt so real … so wonderful." My mother's eyes were moist and twinkling when she told me this story. I think my grandmother's must have been just like that, too, back then in those special moments, her children wiggling and giggling in their beds. Even seven or so decades later, my mother still remembers the little china tea set she got that Christmas.

And as it happened every Christmas morning in my grandmother's house, while the kids peeled and ate the small, white-veined sections of their mandarin oranges and counted out the pieces of hard peppermint candy from their stockings, and my grandfather stoked the fire in the coal stove to keep them all warm, she would be in the kitchen. A Christmas pudding would already be steaming on the stove while she prepared the turkey – probably a crooked-breasted turkey from her flock as it would have been unfit for sale – stuffing it with her savoury French dressing, everyone eager for its fragrant roasting and the day's coming feast.

DARK CHRISTMAS CAKE

12 eggs
4 cups brown sugar
2 pounds butter
1/2 cup sour milk
2 cups molasses
2 teaspoons cloves
2 teaspoons allspice
2 teaspoons cinnamon
1 teaspoon mace

1/2 teaspoon nutmeg
6 cups raisins
1/2 pound mixed peel
3 cups chopped almonds
1 cup flour
1/2 pint fruit juice or wine
1 pint brandy
2 teaspoons baking soda
Flour, as needed

Mix eggs, sugar and butter, and then add molasses, milk and spices. Toss fruit and almonds with 1 cup of flour. Combine the two mixtures. Stir in juice and brandy. Add baking soda and enough flour to make a stiff batter. Pour into pans and bake in a preheated 325 degree oven. For loaf pans, bake 1 hour. For large cake pans, bake up to 3 hours.

WHITE CHRISTMAS CAKE

3 eggs
1 cup white sugar
1 cup butter
1/2 cup almonds
1/2 cup walnuts
1/2 pound glazed cherries
1 cup mixed peel

1/2 cup flour
1 teaspoon brandy
1/2 cup fruit juice
2 cups flour
1 teaspoon baking powder
1/2 teaspoon salt

Mix eggs, sugar and butter well. Toss nuts, cherries and peel with 1/2 cup flour. Combine these two mixtures. Add brandy and juice. Then add remaining ingredients and stir. Pour into large greased loaf pan. Bake in preheated 325 degree oven for 1 hour.

CHOCOLATE ALMOND CAKE

3 squares of baking chocolate	2 cups white sugar
2 1/2 cups flour	5 eggs
1 teaspoon baking soda	1 cup milk or buttermilk
1/4 teaspoon salt	2 teaspoons vanilla
1 cup butter	1 cup chopped almonds

Start melting chocolate in a double boiler. In the meantime, sift flour and add baking soda and salt. In a separate bowl, cream butter and add sugar and eggs, and then blend in melted chocolate. Add the flour mixture, milk, vanilla and nuts. Pour into a greased and floured loaf pan. Bake in a preheated 375 degree oven for approximately 50 minutes.

DATE-FILLED OATMEAL COOKIES

Cookie:

1 cup shortening	1 3/4 cups flour
1 cup brown sugar	3 teaspoons baking powder
1/2 cup milk	Pinch of salt
2 cups oatmeal	

Mix shortening and sugar. Add milk and oatmeal, and mix in remaining dry ingredients to form dough. Roll out on floured surface to 1/4 inch thick and cut in rounds with a cookie cutter. Place on a lightly greased cookie sheet. Bake in a preheated 350 degree oven for 8 to 10 minutes. Let cool before removing from sheet.

Filling:

1 pound dates
1/2 cup brown sugar
2/3 cup water

Cut up dates, add sugar and water. Cook on the stove at medium heat until mixture makes a smooth paste. Cool and spread between two cookies.

TWISTED BREAD DOUGHNUTS

1 1/2 cups milk	1 package active dry yeast
1/4 cup sugar	1 egg, well-beaten
2 teaspoons salt	5 1/2 cups flour
1/4 cup lard	Lard for frying
1 teaspoon sugar	Sugar for rolling
1/2 cup water, lukewarm	

Heat the milk and pour into a large bowl. Add the 1/4 cup sugar, salt and lard, and stir until the lard melts. Let cool to lukewarm.

In the meantime, dissolve 1 teaspoon of sugar into the 1/2 cup of water and sprinkle the mixture with the yeast. Let stand for 10 minutes, then stir and add to the milk mixture. Add the egg and stir well. Beat 3 cups of flour into the liquid, then add 2 more cups, and work the final bit of flour into the dough with your hands. Knead until smooth and elastic, approximately 5 minutes.

Place the dough in a bowl and grease the top of it lightly. Cover and let rise in a warm place until double in size, approximately 1 1/2 hours.

Cut off a portion of the dough with a knife, form it into a ball, and roll out on a floured surface to about 1/2 inch thick. Cut the dough into 3 inch by 5 inch squares, and then cut two lengthwise slits, spaced evenly apart, in each square. Take dough of outside edge of one slit, fold it over and pull the dough from the opposite outside slit through the opening to knot the square together. Immediately drop the piece into the pot of hot lard. Brown both sides of the doughnut, remove to a towel to drain off the fat, and then roll in sugar. Let cool. Repeat process with each square of dough.

These doughnuts freeze well. Take directly out of the granary (or freezer), put on a baking sheet in a preheated 325 degree oven for a few minutes. Test for softness and serve.

FUDGE

2 cups white sugar	1/4 cup light or dark corn syrup
1/4 cup butter	1/2 cup milk
1 cup brown sugar	2 tablespoons cocoa

Mix all ingredients in a saucepan. Bring to a boil and cook until a soft ball forms when dropped in cold water. Remove from heat and beat the mixture until thick. Pour into a buttered pan. Cool and cut into squares.

With the modern convenience of a cooking thermometer, the "soft ball" stage of this recipe could be measured at 235°F but, historically, no one in our family ever used one to decide when the mixture was ready to remove from the heat. The most interesting part of making this recipe is trying to figure out what a soft ball actually looks and feels like, which clearly means that the fudge can end up in various consistencies, depending on the cook. In my memory, a small dollop in cold water looked like a descending brown glob in a lava lamp and felt like a nicely chewed piece of bubble gum. But then, my fudge turned out gooey; the kind you scoop and eat off a spoon. Needless to say, this was nothing like my grandmother's creamy, yet solid, squares of confection.

PEANUT BRITTLE

2 cups white sugar
1 cup (or so) shelled roasted peanuts

Spread peanuts in a buttered pan. Melt 2 cups white sugar in a heavy saucepan over low heat. Stir constantly until sugar is completely melted. Pour over peanuts and let cool. Break into pieces.

WHITE CANDY

2 cups white sugar
1 cup white corn syrup
1/2 cup cold water
A few drops of maple flavouring

Bring sugar, syrup and water to a boil for 7 minutes, stirring constantly, adding maple flavouring at about the 5 minute mark. Continue stirring until quite thick. Drop by the teaspoonful on to wax paper and quickly press walnut halves into top of each candy. This candy hardens quickly, so you have to work fast.

CHRISTMAS PUDDING

2 eggs
1 cup white sugar
1 cup milk
1 cup bread crumbs
1 cup chopped suet
1/2 cup molasses
1/2 cup brandy

1/2 cup raisins
1/2 cup walnuts
2 cups flour
2 teaspoons allspice
2 teaspoons cloves
1 teaspoon cinnamon
1/2 teaspoon salt

Mix eggs, sugar and milk; add crumbs, suet and molasses. Mix in brandy, raisins and walnuts. Then add dry ingredients. Pour mixture into a heat-safe bowl or an empty coffee tin. Set inside a cooking pot containing 2 to 3 inches of water. Place on top of the stove, cover and steam for 2 hours.

Keep warm on stove top until ready to use. Spoon into serving sizes and top with butter sauce.

Butter Sauce for pudding:

5 tablespoons brown sugar
1 tablespoon flour
3 tablespoons butter
1 1/2 cups boiling water

Mix first three ingredients together in a pot on the stove. Add boiling water. Cook slowly on low heat for a few minutes until slightly thickened. Spoon over pudding.

GRAMMA'S FRENCH DRESSING
(Poultry Stuffing)

4–5 large potatoes, cooked,
   drained and riced
8 soda crackers, crushed
4–5 slices of white bread,
   cubed
1 teaspoon cinnamon (approx.)
1/2 teaspoon nutmeg

1/4 teaspoon cloves
1/2 medium onion, chopped
Salt and pepper, to taste
Water, as needed
3 tablespoons butter, softened

Mix first eight ingredients together in a large bowl. Slowly add water until the mixture sticks together (not crumbly). Add the butter gradually and continue to mix. Stuff chicken or turkey and roast.

If extra dressing is left over after stuffing, put in foil and roast with poultry for the last hour of cooking, making sure to squirt a little of the roasting juice into it once or twice during that time.

Sooner or later
you get it right

"Gramma, would you teach us how to make tourtière?" My sister Elaine mangled the beautiful French word for meat pie. But I could do no better, as none of our generation has learned to speak the language of our heritage. Of the three girls, Elaine is the oldest and often elected to speak on our behalf because she is both assertive and wily, as first children often are. But when she made her inquiry, she still sounded like a little girl. We all feel gastronomically small in the presence of our grandmother.

"Sure," she shrugged her shoulders and puckered her lips.

We are in my sister Sylvia's kitchen. Elaine is visiting from her home, then in Qatar, and I, from Arizona. Each summer, when the days are balmy and tumbles of clouds meander through the blue brilliance of unending sky, we make our journeys back to Brandon to spend time with our family – our parents, Sylvia and our two brothers, Ed and Bob. We are farm girls at heart and cannot pass a year without being near the yeasty musk of wheat fields and the purple seas of flax. On this occasion our grandmother is visiting from British Columbia, too.

We conspired beforehand to ask her to give us a lesson in meat pie-making. Not that we had to conspire, as my grandmother has always been generous with her time and willing to share whatever we ask of her. But, we agreed that in order for us to make her tour-tière the way we remember it tasting, there was no other way than to corner her and watch her do it from beginning to end. And we also agreed that this recipe definitely needed to be preserved because it is part of our best memories of her, the savoury pies lined up on the counter as we would sit at the kitchen table sipping cups of Red Rose tea and talking about all manner of things. Never one to monopolize a conversation, she was a good listener, and when we were young that made us feel special. It still does. But if you could get her to talk about her own experiences, she would take you there in serpentine memories, a reflection of her long and varied life.

I learned a lot about my grandmother over cups of tea. That's when I found out that while growing up on a farm in Saskatchewan she gained no experience in the kitchen.

"So how did you learn to cook, Gramma?" I remember asking her.

"Oh, I watch. Every chance I get, I watch."

And now we are here, her three granddaughters, eager to watch her in the kitchen, eager to learn. "We're going to write down your recipe," I say.

"You don't need to write nothing down. It's only a few things," Gramma sputters out the words in a little laugh. Her eyes glitter; her face always bursts into light when she is amused. Of course, the recipes she used didn't come to her in that way. They came from observing out of the corner of her eye while separating milk in her mother's kitchen, and then from the edge of the room in her mother-in-law's home.

"You got some hamburger, dear?" she asks, already up and out of her chair, rubbing the palms of her hands on her hips as if priming them for action.

Sylvia jumps to attention. "Yes, we do, Gramma," her voice sing-songy with excitement, "and what else do you need?"

"A good-sized onion and maybe about six potatoes … and the spices. We start that first and then I make the crusts. So I need some flour and lard, too."

My sister bustles about the kitchen, quickly setting on the counter a frying pan, a cooking pot, three pie plates, a bag of flour and a can of Crisco, before standing at the edge of the U-shaped kitchen like a soldier, hands behind her back, awaiting orders.

In her advancing years, my grandmother doesn't move quickly but every move is deliberate and rhythmic. It feels like we are in the prelude to a song and when her work begins we will be caught up in the melody of it. She begins by lightly sautéing some chopped onion in a bit of butter, then crumbles the ground beef into the pan and stirs and pokes at it so the meat breaks apart into little morsels. Then, her old hands nimbly pare the potatoes.

Elaine and I lean on the outside of the counter that separates the kitchen from the dining area, papers and pencils in hand, both taking notes, which we have decided we will compare later to fine-tune her instructions. We watch quietly.

I clear my throat before I ask, "Was that three pounds of ground beef?"

"Yes, about that. But you could use less and add some pork if you want."

"And you cook it slowly for an hour?"

"About an hour, 'til it get nice and crumbly."

"At medium heat?"

"Or a little lower. You watch it and stir it, make sure it get nice and brown."

I write "nice and crumbly and brown" in brackets next to "medium heat" with a question mark beside it.

"So, Gramma … um, you said six potatoes, right?"

"Yes, dear. But if the potatoes are small maybe you use eight or nine."

In one fluid motion she cuts the last potato into the pot of water, puts it on the stove, turns it up to high, shakes a bit of salt and pepper into the pan of meat and onions, and stirs it briskly.

In unison, Elaine and I put pens to paper: Season meat with salt and pepper. So far she has only used three ingredients but I already have a page of notes.

Sylvia steps tentatively toward the counter. "Do you need anything else, Gramma?" She doesn't have to be tentative in her own kitchen. This is a woman who churns out monstrous meals for four hungry boys every day; she's being respectful of the long-held rhythm of our grandmother's way of moving about her work when she's in the kitchen. The feel of it is perceptible, an almost audible hum. We are watching her performance; we are in the middle of her song.

"No, dear. This is just fine. I think I make the crusts now," she announces in a small voice.

I wonder if she is uncomfortable with all of us leaning in on her, watching her every move, as she has mostly worked alone in the kitchen, maybe as a way of leaving everything behind for a brief hour or two. Or, as I look at her tiny frame, frailer now in her eighties, I am worried that maybe this has been too much to ask of her and she is getting tired.

Her hand dips into the flour bag, then drops the mound into a mixing bowl quickly, deftly – once, twice, how many times?

"Uh, Gramma, how much flour would you say that is?"

She stares into the bowl. "Oh, about four, four and a half, maybe five cups." And then she laughs, "You know I don't use no measure. I use a special bowl and fill it a certainty amount. I been doing that all my life. That bowl, it go everywhere with me."

I know the bowl she speaks of; the middle-sized one of a set of three – thick and milky white inside, pale yellow outside and multi-purpose – which she used for mixing, or serving a dish of cold potato salad, or oven-hot macaroni. I think about all the moves my grand-mother has made, and how deliberately and lovingly she must have packed that bowl, one of the small constants in her continually changing life.

"Like your black, iron pot, eh Gramma?"

"Oh yes, dear. Like my black pot. I cook many a meal in that old, black pot."

She has scooped a couple of hunks of Crisco into the bowl and is working the shortening into the flour with magnificent speed. Her voice shakes a little with her movement, "This stuff don't make such a good pie crust. Lard is better. Pig fat, you know. That's what I use when we were on the farm … yes, that lard make such nice crust."

Her actions flow in a mounting crescendo as she rubs the flour and shortening into a butter-coloured meal and tips a trail of water from a cup into the bowl. Her hands push and move the mixture into dough, her body rocking back and forth with the rhythm. A dusting of flour floats through her fingers onto the counter. And then the rolling pin whirls and spins this way and that, loose but controlled in her grip, pulsing the knob of pastry until it's smooth and thin. Then the gentle flop of crust into a pie tin, more pushing and moving and cutting the edges with a paring knife in a calliope spin. Again and again and again she does this, each crust perfect in its plate.

Sylvia stands with her hands over her mouth, and Elaine and I, our minds twirling, wordlessly try to record her dervish magic. How much shortening did she use? Was that more flour she added, or was it water? How much would that be in cups? Teaspoons? Tablespoons? What?

"Okay," she says, "those potatoes should be done. Do you have a ricer, dear?"

My sister pumps her arms and high-steps her way out of the mesmerizing moment. "Of course, Gramma, but let me do the pota-toes for you," she offers.

My grandmother finally accepts my sister's help, "Oh, all right."

She shakes what she tells us is about one teaspoon or so of cinnamon, about a half teaspoon of nutmeg and the same of cloves, and a little more salt and pepper into the meat and then folds in the fluffy, riced potatoes. She quietly tends to the savoury mixture for a few minutes, stirring and watching, one hand on her hip, then spoons equal amounts into the pastry shells and delicately covers each with a top crust. Moving the pie tin slowly in a counter-clock-wise direction, she uses the palms of her hands to define its edge and, after slicing away the excess dough with a knife, rhythmically presses her thumb and index finger along the edge to seal the crust in fluted beauty. Four quick slashes on the top crust of each pie and into the hot oven. Her song is done.

Our pencils are on the counter. We have recorded the ingredients of the filling for our grandmother's tourtière on paper, but my sisters and I have no idea how we will ever replicate her delectable melt-in-our-mouths crust. When we tell her this she says, "It take me a long time to make a good crust. See, you watch me do it, now you go try. Keep trying." She shrugs and puckers, "Sooner or later, you get it right."

TOURTIÈRE

3 lbs "not too lean" ground beef
1 large onion, chopped
Salt and pepper
6 large potatoes, peeled
1 teaspoon cinnamon
1/2 teaspoon each nutmeg and ground cloves
3 unbaked double pie crusts

Brown meat and onion in a large frying pan; add salt and pepper to taste and cook slowly for about an hour, stirring often so meat doesn't stick to pan.

In the meantime, boil peeled potatoes. When potatoes are cooked, rice them into the meat mixture and add cinnamon, nutmeg, cloves and more salt and pepper to taste. Mix and cook for approximately 15 minutes on low heat, stirring often.

Divide evenly into pie crusts, cover with top crusts, which have been vented, and bake in a preheated 375 degree oven for 45 minutes, or until crusts are nicely browned. Serve immediately. (Extra pies can be cooled and frozen for later use: reheat at 300 degrees for about 1 hour.)

Though this dish was not reserved for Christmas, my maternal great-grandmother Philomène, my grandmother and my mother always served it on Christmas Eve, and made enough extra (kept cooled in the root cellar or frozen in the granary) to heat up and munch on well into the New Year. That lingering fragrance of meat seasoned with cinnamon, nutmeg and cloves and the subtle earthy, smooth scent of baked pie crust will forever be synonymous with the holiday season in my family.

PIE CRUST
(Makes 6 shells or 3 shells and pie tops)

4 cups white flour
2 teaspoons salt
1 pound pork lard (or shortening)
Ice-cold water, as needed

Blend flour and salt in a bowl. Cut up lard and add to flour mixture with a pastry blender until crumbly; then rub mixture between hands to make into even finer texture. Add ice-cold water, 1/4 of a cup at a time until dough is firm. (If the dough is sticky, you have used too much water. Start again.)

Separate enough dough to make one pie crust. On a floured surface, roll out to 1/4 inch thickness with rolling pin. Lift dough delicately but quickly into a pie pan and mold to inside; then cut extra dough from edge of pan. Leftover edges can be used for making next crust.

To make extra pie shells for other use, bake at 400 degrees for 30 minutes.

My grandmother obviously had a magic touch when it came to making pie crusts. (Personally, I've cried, cursed, mostly given up and called on my good friend Sara Lee to make one that isn't chewy or hard as stone.) And even more wondrous: she could make a batch in minutes. This recipe is as close as my mother and I could come to recording her magic. I wish you peace and joy, should you decide to try it.

Use everything but the squeak and the tail

HAM

Butcher a pig in the spring.

Take the big parts of the hind and fore legs and hang them in a cool place, such as a root cellar. Once a week, for four weeks, brush the legs thoroughly with Smokine (liquid smoke) and, at the same time, inject Smokine into the thickest parts of the meat using a syringe.

Wrap the hams in heavy paper, put in large gunny sacks and store in the granary in the wheat until needed.

"Dad would get one of the neighbours or Uncle Henri to come and help do the butchering," my mother says. "Mom was there, of course, but the pig was too big for her to handle alone with Dad … now, this is the terrible part … he stuck it in the neck with a knife to kill it. That's when Mom collected the blood to make her sausage … blood sausage was a delicacy back then."

BLOOD SAUSAGE

Drain blood from butchered pig into a large bucket

4 cups fresh blood
2 cups ground pork
1 medium onion, chopped
Salt and pepper

Mix all ingredients together. Pour into a 9 inch square baking pan and cook in a preheated 375 degree oven for approximately 30 minutes. Cut into squares and serve.

"After Dad killed the pig, they bound the hind legs and raised it by a pulley looped on one of the barn rafters, and then when all the blood was drained, they dipped the pig into a big tub of hot water … that made it easy to scrape all the hair off the skin … and, of course, then they started the butchering. Mom used everything but the squeak … that's what she called the snout … and the tail. That gave us meat way into October, November, until they slaughtered a cow." When she says this, my mother laughs a little and shrugs her shoulders, just as my grandmother would have.

SALT PORK

Side of pork from freshly butchered pig
Salt

Cut the fatter part of the side into six inch squares. Rub thoroughly with salt. Put pieces in a stone crock and press them together tightly. Cover crock with a plate weighted down with a big stone and put in a cool place, such as the root cellar. After about 3 weeks the meat makes a brine, at which time it is ready to use.

Take out one or two squares from the crock and replace the plate and stone. Slice the meat and parboil it in water to remove most of the salt. Fry slices in a cast iron frying pan, adding a bit of ground pepper, until they are nice and brown and crispy. Serve.

"The rind gets crispy when it's cooked, so you have to crunch it and chew on it to eat it ... it tasted so good. Seems odd, I know, but we all just loved it when Mom fried up a batch of side pork."

HEADCHEESE

1 head and 4 hocks (feet) from freshly butchered pig
1 medium onion, sliced
Salt and pepper, to taste

Remove ears, eyes, snout and skin from pig's head. Discard these. Cut head into four pieces. Remove skin from pig's feet up to the hocks and discard. Cut feet into pieces.

Rinse all pieces in cold water and put in a large pot on the stove, adding onion, salt and pepper, with enough water to cover. Bring to a boil, then lower heat and simmer for approximately 4 hours. Stir often so meat does not stick to the bottom of the pot. Keep adding water so the meat does not brown or burn, or so that the mixture does not become too thick. Cook until all the meat falls off the bones.

Remove all the bones. Divide mixture into small containers making sure each includes some of the jelly. Let cool. Slice and serve.

"People always shudder when I talk about headcheese, but, honestly, it was delicious. Mom made it quite often, even after she left the farm ... I still make it once in a while, too ... you get a craving for these kinds of things, you know. Of course, you can't find a pig's head like we used on the farm, but you can buy pork hocks at the store. They make a good jelly, and then all those little bones are so nice to suck on ... what a treat."

LARD

From a freshly butchered pig, remove all fat from its skin and sectioned pieces, such as roasts and hams. Cut fat into cubes, put in a big iron pot and cook slowly until the cubes are crisp. Drain the fat into a stone crock and store in a cool place, such as the root cellar. Use lard for making pie crusts and other baked goods.

"Mom always said that pig lard was best for baking, especially pie crusts. And, you know, no one could make a pie crust like her!"

SAUSAGE

1 pound ground pork
1 pound ground beef
1 medium onion, finely chopped
1 teaspoon allspice (or more, to taste)
Salt and pepper, to taste

Combine all ingredients, mixing well. Put through a press into casing (well cleaned pig intestines) to form sausages or make patties with hands. Fry and serve, or put in layers in a stone crock, cover with melted lard and store in a cool place for later use.

"Making sausage was quite a process. She had to clean all the junk out of the intestines; she'd scrape and wash them for hours until they were good and clean … even turned them inside out to make sure there wasn't a speck of poop left anywhere … and then she soaked them in salted water until she needed them, which was never too long, I assure you, because all that fresh meat had to get processed as soon as possible."

CANNED MEAT

Clean canning sealers (Mason jars)
Pork or beef, uncooked
Salt and pepper, to taste

Cut meat into cubes and pack into sealers. Put 1/2 teaspoon each of salt and pepper into each jar. Put sealed jars into a large container of water on the stove and bring to a boil. Cook for three hours at a continual boil. The meat will produce its own juice as it cooks, so be careful when removing the jars from the container. Tighten lids and let cool. Store in a cool place, such as the root cellar.

Please note: As food safety and knowledge has improved over the decades, so has knowledge of the dangers of home canning, such as the risk of botulism. If attempting this recipe, please first consult a reputable source for safety guidelines such as Health Canada.

"Mom would always cook a nice pork roast after the butchering, but she canned most of the loin meat. We had no refrigeration back then, so that was the only way to preserve meat through the summer, other than smoking it."

PRESSED PORK

Pork hocks with lots of meat on them
or 1 whole chicken, cut in pieces
1 medium onion, chopped
Salt and pepper, to taste

Remove skin from pork hocks or chicken. Put in an iron pot. Add onion, seasoning and enough water to cover the meat. Bring to a boil and then lower heat to a simmer, adding water occasionally to keep a nice thickness to the meat. Stir often and cook 3 to 4 hours, until meat falls off the bones. Remove from heat and remove all bones. Put meat in small containers and let cool. Fat will come to the surface and can be removed. Slice and serve.

As my mother recalls the butchering process, I feel remarkably removed from my grandmother's experience. Yes, I've eaten home-cured ham and sausage; I've sucked on the leftover bones from making headcheese and gratifyingly chewed on the rinds of cooked salt pork (though I've never partaken of a fresh, blood sausage meal). To this day I prefer homemade pressed pork or chicken, rather than deli meats purchased from the store. But I am a little ashamed to say that I have no desire to slip into my grandmother's shoes and do the arduous work of her hands when it comes to the blood and guts of butchering. Instead, I work hard just to keep my awareness of the rhythm – the give and take – of life and death and try to sort out the difference between need and want.

Looking at memory

At close to 90 years old, Marie-Anne still looked vibrant and stylish.

My grandfather, Isaie Lacaille, at 16 years old, 1915.

The Fradette family, shortly after coming to Saskatchewan, standing in front of their home. Left to right: Adélard, Marie-Anne, Aydelie, Marie, Joseph, Albert, Napoléon, Philomène, Ferdinand and Edmond. Henri and Emile are standing in front.

The Fradette family, taken shortly after their new two-storey house was built on the Saskatchewan homestead.

Ferdinand's application for the Saskatchewan homestead. Note that he has signed his name "Fradette" rather than "Fradet" after his ancestor, Jean. The family genealogist, Julien Fradette, says that this likely came about in response to the often-used pronunciation of the final "t" by Anglos, but that many descendents are now returning to the original spelling of the name.

Audelie and Marie-Anne, at about 12 and 10 years old, wearing their Sunday best, 1912.

Marie-Anne and Audelie in the field with their wagon and team of horses, likely bringing coffee and sandwiches to the threshing crew.

The Soda Lake School, where at least two generations of Lacaille children attended, still stands. Photo taken in 2007.

Marie-Anne (on the left) and Audelie dressed for a typical day of chores on the farm.

Some of the many cows my grandmother milked and tended to over the years.

Philomène and Ferdinand,
ages 48 and 51, 1914.

Teenagers, Audelie
and Marie-Anne, in
front of their parents'
home, dressed up and
likely on the way to a
party or dance, circa
1917.

April the 4th, Sunday School re-opened, officers appointed: Supt. Mr. A. F. McKague, Asst. Supt. Mr. John Bebensee, Treas. Mr. W. E. White Sect. Mr. J. Bothwell, and Asst. Mrs. N. Eden. The teachers as last year. A good attendance on the first Sunday speaks well for the coming months.

On Tuesday March the 29th, Messrs. Henry and Isaac Lachille gave a very pleasant party to their friends and neighbors, to give all an opportunity of meeting their brides. The grooms received the guests, and the brides looked most charming with circlets of orange blossom in their hair and wearing dainty suits with white crepe over blouses. Mr. H. Reid, of Ogema, was master of ceremonies. Introductions over the neighbors passed in a circle, by the two happy couples, wishing them every joy. Following this a jolly few hours were spent, when the luncheon was served by the mother of the bridegrooms. All enjoyed the bountiful spread and after a few dances the evening was concluded. The brides each received a silver pyrex pie plate as a slight token of good wishes from their near neighbors present during the evening.

Isaie and Marie-Anne on their wedding day, February 22, 1921.

Newlyweds Isaie and Marie-Anne, on the left; Audelie and Henri on the right.

Isaie's mother, Soufrine, in her later years. Born May 11, 1862 and died three years after her husband, on October 5, 1944.

Isaie's father, Louis Lacaille, taken in his later years – lawyer, homesteader – born November 2, 1860; died December 8, 1941.

A winter scene of Marie-Anne and Isaie's home on the farm.

Marie-Anne and Isaie with their first child, my mother, Florence, 1926.

The farmyard, which remained much the same as it was in the 1920s when my grandparents first moved there, 1960.

A current view of the Lacaille farmland, 2008.

My grandmother's buggy and team of horses, which she used to take meals to the men in the fields and often to go to town to deliver her butter and eggs to Jack Seede's store.

Isaie purchased a Model T car in the mid 1920s. It may well have been turned into the Bennett wagon they used with a team of horses during the Depression years.

Mom & Dad

Isaie on top of the haystack; Marie-Anne standing on the wagon. This scene is similar to the one in which my grandmother got knocked on the head with a piece of metal used for securing the stack.

Hay bales in the field as we see them today. A long way from my grandparents' view of the harvested land.

My grandmother's iron pot, which is now in the safe keeping of my Aunt Helen's daughter, Sharon.

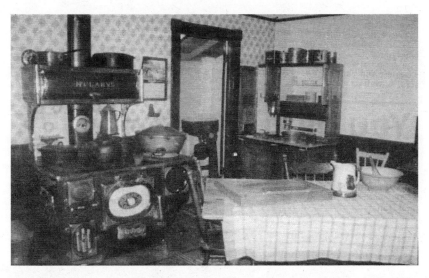

This McClary's stove, found here in a replica of a pioneer kitchen, is similar to the one Marie-Anne used on the farm.

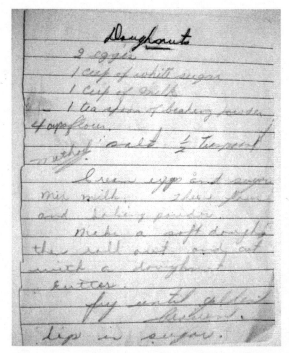

This is one of only two recipes known to be written in my grandmother's hand, offered to Ernie's wife, Betty, well over 55 years ago in the newlyweds' kitchen one Saturday morning, when mother-in-law and daughter-in-law were baking together.

An example of a rag rug, woven by my mother, Florence, as taught to her by my grandmother, Marie-Anne.

My grandmother in front of the big
red house on Sixth Street in Brandon.

Marie-Anne at her 95th "No Mens" birthday party in Regina.

You got to learn to be patient

Regardless of the time or place, my grand-parents, my mother, and aunts and uncles talked often about their lives on the farm. Their recollections would move easily from one to another at family dinners, or while shuffling cards during games of canasta, or in response to my never-ending questions. Over the years, their stories have become the lore that keeps me close to my roots and are now so much a part of me that my family's memories meld with my own, our mutual love of the land, resonant and so real.

It is easy to imagine my grandmother back in the late 1930s as she sat on her three-legged stool in the barn and squeezed the cow's teats, one-two, one-two, fast and even, the warm milk making bubbly foam in the pail, then pausing for a moment to wipe her brow. The Holstein would be the last of several she had milked that morning. I see it looking back at her with a wary cow look, trying to swoosh its tail, and her, smiling with a shake of her finger as if to say, you're not going to get me this time. She would have tied its tail to its hind leg so it couldn't whip fresh dung in her face. My grandmother had a long history with cows and knew that milking could be precar-ious at times. She looked down through wire-rimmed glasses at her husband's speckled grey wool sock on her right foot as she contin-ued the whoosh-whoosh of milking, the pail inching full.

"Well, that cow, she not quite used to me," my grandmother told me. "When I go to milk her, she kick her hind leg out and it get me in the foot. Oh, it hurt like hell and it swell pretty bad but I could still move my toes, so I'm pretty sure it wasn't broke," she shrugged her shoulders, "when I finish the milking I go back to the house and put some liniment on it and wrap it in a towel. Then I put one of your grampa's big socks on it … it was too swoll up to put my boot back on, you see." She sat back in her chair and folded her arms, matter-of-factly, across her middle, "Then I just go back out and finish the rest of my chores."

The air in the barn would have been dense from the previous night's rain; the smell of hay and manure, pungent in her nose. Life was returning to the land at the end of that decade. The fields were thick with ripening wheat; and her garden grew lush again, swaying in a gentle response to a wisp of the early morning breeze – lettuce and turnip leaves, feathery carrot tops, the purple hue of beet greens; white-flowered potato foliage and waist-high columns of corn; a low sea of cucumber and pumpkin plants, their blossoms riding waves of leaves overlapping like hands folded in contentment; and a great fountain of rhubarb stood regal in one corner. Everything held the promise of sufficiency once more, maybe even prosperity. Finally, my grandmother could try to forget the Depression's dry summers when the garden was barren except for a short row of wilting lettuce she tried to nurture to life with what little water could be spared from the well.

I can see her rising from milking and untying the cow's tail from its leg. "That's a good girl," she said, running her hand down its white and black spotted haunch. The cow stirred with a low groan of a moo. She picked up a full, heavy pail of milk in each hand; there were still three more to carry to the house. She could hear her sons' voices rise and fall in laughter, and called out to them, "Ernie. Edward. Come here, help me carry the milk." The two boys, thirteen and eleven, stumbled into the barn, their faces no doubt flushed from play. They said nothing, just looked at one another and laughed, picked up the pails and started toward the house. During the summer the farm was their giant playground, and they liked its freedom, away from all the book learning and lessons of school. Every year come September, my grandmother had to rein them in with a good talking to. "You got to go school. It's important to learn," she would say.

And every fall, my Uncle Ernie replied, "I hate school. I don't learn nothin'," while Edward just grinned. He liked school, just as my mother, Florence, did, but he wouldn't contradict Ernie. They were a team.

"Yes, I had a terrible time keeping track of those two boys," my grandmother recalled, her shoulders quivering as she let out her familiar half-laugh, half-giggle. "Sometime they show up, their overalls just black and all ripped on the knees … every week I have to mend those damn pants … and I say to them, 'What you two been up to?' but," she shrugged, "of course, they don't tell me." The smile left her face, "I always worry about Ernie, you know, maybe he trip and fall and get hurt real bad … but he never like to listen to me when I tell him to be careful."

Ernie and Edward would have set their pails of milk on the table by the separator in the shanty, a small built-on room at the entrance to the house. My grandmother glanced through the open door into the kitchen as she set her pails next to theirs. The two were at the kitchen table next to Eva and Helen, waiting patiently for breakfast. Florence, my mother, sat with them, arms folded in front of her, head stooped over an open book, her shoulder-length blond hair pulled away from her face with straight combs. She was a slim girl, with dancing, crystal blue eyes, who could shine a full-lipped, toothy smile to make young men look twice and ask for second dances.

"I always had my nose in a book," my mother tells me when I asked her what she and my aunts and uncles did for fun on those long summer days of no school, miles away from other children. She smiles just as I imagine she did when she was that sweet-faced sixteen-year-old. "Read – that's what I liked to do. Eva and Helen, they liked to play with the cat, dress it up and pretend it was a baby. And the boys, well, they played 'horse and man' … one would be the horse, with a rope tied around his waist, and the other would be the man; the man got to direct the horse to go wherever he wanted … then they'd switch. It was nothing, really, but they played like that for hours on end. Of course, that was when there were no chores to do. Me, I always helped with the separating … and then I had to clean that awful machine … morning and night."

As she did every day, my grandmother set aside a pail of milk for that day's use and then poured another into a container, with a screen covering its top, to strain out bits of dirt or debris. She re-poured the strained milk into the separator's metal barrel and began turning the long handle attached to the side of the machine, around and around, her feet planted firmly on the floor to stabilize herself, her entire body swaying in a smooth, methodical way.

My grandfather walked in, smiling. He always seemed to be smiling, even when there was nothing to smile about. "Looks like the cows give a lot this morning, eh?" he said as he strode into the kitchen and sat down at the table and then stared in mock contemplation toward the ceiling, "I'll be extra nice when I bed them down tonight. I'll sing them a song."

"Mmm …" my grandmother murmured. Her husband's natural joie de vivre annoyed her at times, but it was the thing that charmed her when they first met, made her feel buoyant in a hard life that felt like it was slipping under water. She looked at him as she continued to crank the separator handle. He had not lost his youthful stature as some of the other men had, still as lean and sinewy as when she first laid eyes on him twenty years before. But his thick thatch of dark hair, untamed on top – a bit like a haystack – had hints of grey on the close-shaved temples; his smooth-featured face with its long, straight nose had weathered into a dark tan, and tiny lines spread from the corners of his wide, still-curious eyes.

The cream began to flow slowly from one of the separator's spouts into a clean can while skimmed milk from the other went back into the empty milk pail. "Okay, Florence, you take over now." My grandmother poured another bucket into the screened pail, tipped it carefully into the separator barrel and then went to the kitchen to serve her hungry brood homemade bread with bowls of the morning's fresh milk.

"We have a busy day today. I'm making butter. So Helen, Eva, I need your help," my grandmother said.

The two nodded; their small faces, serious. As the youngest, four and eight years old, their job was to sit on the lid of the churn to keep it in place while their mother or one of the older children turned the handle.

"Boys, I need you, too, once you come back from getting water with Papa," she said as she poured her husband a cup of coffee.

"More bread, please?" Ernie called out. Edward, smiling slyly, had already taken the last slice.

My grandfather stirred a large pour of cream into his cup and spread a thick layer of butter on a slice of bread and then dunked it in his coffee, scooting the mixture into his mouth before a single caramel-coloured crumb could be left behind. He smiled, lips together, the bread bulging from one cheek. The children watched him, fascinated by their father's morning ritual. Though Ernie was two years older, the boys could have passed for twins: close in size with long thin faces and high foreheads, and smiles that lit their blue eyes with that familiar, prankish glint. But Ernie's demeanour, like my grandmother's, was always more serious, determined, maybe as a result of the palsy in his right arm and leg, a physical burden since birth.

"So, Mama, she make butter today. You know what that mean, eh?" My grandfather spoke loudly, as if to a gathering much larger than the one before him. "Buttermilk. A drink fit for a king." My grandmother laughed as the children contorted their faces in disgust. Tart, cold, in a large cup and sprinkled with salt and pepper, fresh buttermilk was his favourite drink. "What? You don't like a king's drink? … Oh well, that much more for me," he shrugged and winked at Eva and Helen. "Come on, boys, we better go so you come back and help your mama with that churning. My mouth, it watering already."

Ernie stuffed the rest of a piece of bread into his mouth, leaving a sprinkling of crumbs on the table, then put his bowl to his lips and gulped down the remaining milk. Edward was already out the door, eager to get the place next to his father in the Bennett wagon so he could take the reins and guide the team of horses to the spring a few miles down the road. Ernie stumbled from the chair, knocking it to the floor, and scrambled after his brother, his voice trailing back to the kitchen, "I want to be next to Papa, Edward!"

My grandfather shook his head, his face suddenly somber.

"Let him do it, Isaie," my grandmother's tone was soft but firm, almost challenging.

"He don't stand solid. And with that bum arm of his? What if …?"

"*Mon Dieu*, let him try."

He grunted, got up from the table and walked out the door. The two little ones looked at each other and then to their mother.

"Is Papa mad?" Eva puckered her face, bottom lip protruding.

My grandmother exchanged glances with my mother who quietly cleaned the separator parts in the washtub.

"Oh, they never agreed about Ernie. I don't know if Dad was afraid for him or if he felt guilty … or ashamed. I never could figure it out. And he wouldn't talk about it. Not to me, anyway." My mother is quiet for a moment, her arms folded across her middle, her feet delicately crossed at the ankles, a posture so familiar – my grandmother's posture. "My dad was such a carefree sort of guy but when it came to Ernie … well …" she takes a deep breath and shakes her head. "When Ernie was little, Dad found out that there was another boy who lived around us who had the same sort of problem … his family, they had some money, I guess, and took him to a clinic in Regina … and when he came back his leg was almost normal. So Dad decided he'd go see this family to find out what they did to make him better. Oh boy, Mom didn't want him to do that. I don't know if she didn't want to draw more attention to Ernie or maybe she was embarrassed that they couldn't afford to send him to a place like that, but Dad went anyway …

"He came home and told Mom, 'Lay him on the table and move his legs like a bicycle. Every night we have to do it.' So every night Mom did what he said … with Ernie struggling and crying the whole time … and Dad would stand there saying, 'Keep going, keep going.' For months and months he made her do that. It was awful, plain awful. I'll never forget it."

"Come on now, finish your milk, then we go to the barn to feed the pigs," I can hear my grandmother say. While Eva and Helen slurped their bowls, she retrieved the crock of cottage cheese she had started the day before from the back of the stove and poured it into a flour sack, which was draped in a pail to catch the first drops of whey. Then the three of them trailed out the door, like a hen and two chicks, just in time to see Edward standing next to his father on the wood platform of the Bennett wagon at the reins of the two-horse team. The rubber tires of the car chassis rolled a faint cloud of dust on the road. Ernie sat away from them, barely visible behind the metal that, in better years, was the body of a Model T. The sun was already warm in the morning's light breeze. With one hand shading her eyes in a weary salute, my grandmother watched them until they disappeared over the hill. She swallowed hard, trying to push down the frustration that, I expect, wanted to rise up into tears, and then stooped to gather the bag of cheese out of the pail and secure it with clothespins on the line. She watched the whey ooze slowly through the fabric into the pail below.

"I don't know what to do after Ernie was born ... I cry and cry over that ... you know, I come down sick with that fever, rheumatic fever they call it, when I carry him ... I think maybe the fever cause him to be cripple." The few times my grandmother spoke to me of Ernie's condition this is all she would say, the pain of her heart clear in her eyes. To tell her otherwise, that there is no medical evidence to support that rheumatic fever could cause harm to a child in the womb, was futile. She had convinced herself of her blame.

"One time she told me that when she was pregnant with Ernie, her and Dad were fighting a lot about buying more land," my mother says. "Our land was all hills and stones. It was good for pasture but really hard to get any decent crops from it ... so a farm came up for sale, right next to ours ... beautiful, flat land, good for wheat. Mom wanted to buy it, but well, Dad, you know he didn't care about having more land, he thought we were fine with what we had. That made Mom so mad. She said she called him all kinds of names, told him he was stupid and stubborn and really pushed him ... well, finally he agreed, but she said it was a terrible time ... that some-times she thought that all that strife caused Ernie to come out the way he did ... can you believe that? She carried so much suffering about Ernie."

The piglets snorted and snuffled toward her as she entered the stall and poured a pail of skim milk from the morning's separation into the trough. Eva and Helen stayed back, frightened by the animals' quick movements. My grandmother would coddle and attend to the pigs until the next spring when, usually in March or April, one would be butchered for meat.

"Mama, look." Helen held out a chicken egg. "Those chickens are laying in here again," she said with grown-up consternation.

"Well, let's gather them then." My grandmother retrieved a pail from one of the stalls, and the girls began the hunt. They scouted the nooks and crannies of the barn, carrying one egg at a time to set tenderly in the pail at their mother's feet. She counted them under her breath, fifteen eggs. With the gathering she would do later, she'd have more than enough to fill five, twenty-five-egg flats to make a full crate – a good number to sell in town on Saturday and still have some left over for the family. "Okay, little ones, you do a good job. Now back to the house. We got butter to churn."

"Our neighbour, Alfred Larsen, he make me a special churn. Most of them, they only hold a gallon or two of cream. Mine, it hold five gallons," my grandmother explained, a little bit of pride tipping her humble talk. "And your grampa, he make me a wood stamp with my initials 'ML' on it that I press into the butter when I make it into pounds. The man who run the grocery store in town, Jack Seede was his name, he ask me to do that so people who come to buy my butter know for sure it's mine." With her hands clasped together in her lap, she rubbed the back of one hand with the thumb of the other, moving the papery skin this way and that. "I make sixteen, maybe seventeen pounds of butter to sell every week."

She was setting the tub on its four-legged stand in the shanty when Ernie came in the door, his head hanging mournfully.

"Oh, you're back already. Good, we got to start on this butter. Can you help your sister and me get the cream from the cellar?"

"I guess so."

"Where's Edward?"

"Edward's taking the horses to the barn."

"And Papa?"

He frowned and took a deep breath, ready to complain. She knew what was festering inside her son, that he wanted to cry, "He won't let me drive!" but then …

"I'm here," my grandfather said simply. He teetered a bit as he carried two buckets full of water past them into the kitchen; my grandmother followed, and Ernie, after her. He set the water next to the wash table, poured a bucket into the drinking pail and then dipped a cup into it and gulped it down, tilting his head back theatrically. He wiped his mouth on the sleeve of his shirt and let out an exaggerated, "Aaahh. Good," his smile, impish and innocent.

My grandmother ignored him. She would have ignored him just as she felt he had ignored their son's feelings. "Ernie, open the door to the cellar, *s'il te plaît?* Get the cream up here."

"I'll do that," my grandfather said.

"No. Ernie can do it." She looked hard at her husband, her eyes unblinking, accusing, daring him to say otherwise. "I checked on the pigs; they're ready to move to the pen. Go do that."

Ernie lowered himself carefully down the cellar steps, and looked up at his father before his head disappeared.

"But … I …" my grandfather began.

"Let me be. Ernie and Florence will help. Just go."

"You need me, Mama?" My mother appeared from the living room, book in hand.

My grandfather shrugged and disappeared out the door into the yard, whistling a jaunty tune.

"Oh yes, you always knew when Mom was put out about something. She'd get crabby and huff around and then just quit talking. Us kids would stay out of her way, but Dad, he'd just act like nothing was wrong … sometimes, if things got too much for her, she'd drop everything, go in the bedroom and have a real good cry."

Ernie's body rocked, his head down and left arm rolling with the churn's handle. Eva and Helen sat on the lid, legs dangling, heads bobbling to the rhythm of his steady pace. The longer he churned the more difficult the turning became as the liquid spun out of the thickening butter.

"I'll do it now," my mother offered.

Ernie looked up at her; his cheeks flushed in rosy circles and a tiny glisten of sweat banded his smooth forehead.

"You go play until it's time to eat," my grandmother encouraged him as she replaced the full buttermilk container with an empty one.

He wiped his sleeve over his brow with a wide, exaggerated sweep, "Okay, Mama," and sauntered out the door.

"The butter's nearly ready." My mother continued to wind the churn's handle with as much force as her petite frame would have been able to muster.

"I know. Ernie did a good job." I imagine my grandmother smiling the kind of smile that gleamed with satisfaction. She carried the crock of buttermilk to the kitchen cellar where it would cool until she fetched some for her husband's midday meal.

My mother cranked the churn's handle until it would no longer make a full circle and groaned to a stop. Then my grandmother lifted Helen and Eva from their perch. "And you do a good job, too … away you go," she said, petting their blond heads like two kittens and shooing them out the door to play. She removed the churn's lid and scooped the butter, its colour a shade of white with just a hint of yellow, into the large metal bowl she also used for mixing bread dough. Hunched over, pressing with her full weight, she worked the butter with her hands, squeezing and pushing out as much excess water from it as possible. After draining off the liquid, she covered the bowl with a tea towel and put it in the cellar where it would rest overnight. The next day, very early, when the air was cool and the prairie breeze carried the meadowlark's clear song through the open, kitchen window, she would rework it again.

"Yes ... I finish making my butter every Friday. You have to add salt to it and work it until a certainty amount of water comes out and then it's ready. I use a wood box your grampa make for me to make it into pounds. I put some butter in the box and press it down with that piece of wood that have my initials in it ... then I tap it out of there and wrap it in some special wax paper. I put all those pounds in a tub and then your grampa, he put it down in the well to keep it cool until we take it to town. I have to make my butter on Friday ... because I have too much to do on Saturday ... I used to do all my baking on Saturday, you know."

My grandmother stood, hands on her hips, in the cellar, a large, hand-dug earthen hole beneath the kitchen. The air would have been cool and thick with the damp, musty mixture of smells – potatoes, carrots and other root vegetables stored in a bed of sand in one area, and coal for the winter furnace in another. She scanned the shelves my grandfather had built in the corner next to the ladder-style steps where she kept homemade canned goods and her weekly baking. She chose a large Mason jar of canned pork, reached up out of the square hole and placed it on the kitchen floor, and then eased her way up the cellar steps with a dozen potatoes cradled in her apron, and on top of that, a loaf of bread, the second to last of the week's baking. With only one loaf left in the cellar, my grandmother would have to make bread the next day as well as finish the butter.

She was about to begin peeling the potatoes when she heard a piercing cry coming from outside. My mother, who was cleaning the churn in the shanty, ran out the door first with my grandmother following on her heels. Edward staggered toward them from the barnyard, holding his arm, crying in an eerie howl, "I ... I fell. Ooooh, my arm hurts ... Mama, my arm ..."

"Mama, Mama! Edward, Edward!" Eva and Helen, who had been playing in the yard, scattered and circled amidst them like scared chickens. My mother attempted to gather the little girls into her arms as my grandmother tried to peel back the sleeve of her son's shirt.

"Ouch, ouch, ouch, don't touch it!"

"You have to let me look."

Edward closed his eyes and contorted his face as his mother unbuttoned the long-sleeved cuff of his shirt.

"Mon Dieu! What did you do?"

"I fell off the calf."

"You were riding the calf?" She gingerly gathered the sleeve at his upper arm to reveal a sizable bump protruding like a deformed egg from his forearm.

Edward didn't answer. He was looking at his arm through one squinted eye.

"It looks broke. We need to get to the doctor," she said. "Where's Isaie? Where's your papa?"

"I don't know," he moaned.

My grandmother stood for a moment, her hand resting on her chest as if to settle the rapid beating of her heart, when she noticed Ernie peeking around the corner of the barn.

"Ernie, come here!"

He shuffled toward her, head down.

She asked Edward, "Did he ride the calf, too?"

"Ernie, he …" Edward fell silent. His eyes welled with a new batch of tears.

"Stupide. Stupide garçons," she shook her head. Her eyes darted from one child to the next, then toward the barn, to the house and back to Edward's arm. Her voice edged in panic, she started to holler out with all her might, "Help! Help! I need help!"

"I think she was hoping Dad would hear her, but it was George Wagner who heard her yell," my mother remembers. "He lived maybe half a mile northwest of us. It's unbelievable that he actually heard her from his place, but it wasn't very long before he came driving up … he took her and Edward to the doctor in his car … you know, we didn't have a car at that time. Even if Dad had been around, it would have been a long, hard ride by horse and buggy with that broken arm … eleven miles to Radville."

The sun sat low on the horizon by the time they pulled back into the farmyard. My grandfather strode in giant, hurried steps from the pigpen to greet them. He held out his hand to my grandmother as she stepped stiffly from the car, having had her long-legged son nestled in a deep sleep next to her all the way home. Then, he gently ushered Edward, bleary-eyed and holding his casted arm, from the seat, "Come on now, boy. You be okay. Let's go."

My mother rushed toward them from the house, kitchen towel in hand. "Mama, is Edward all right? We've been so worried."

"Yes, he's fine … everything be fine."

My grandfather side-glanced my grandmother and then rounded the car, extending his hand to George, "Well, you got some good ears there, George. My girl here, say Marie-Anne, she yelled something awful, but I was out in the south field … didn't hear a darn thing. Thank you. Thank you very much."

My grandmother recalled, "Oh, that was a hard ride to town … all the time I think, 'Where'd Isaie go and what we going to do? We got no money to pay that doctor.' I'm not going to ask George for no money … but Dr. Crane, he fix up Edward's arm and he say not to worry, he take some of my butter and eggs in trade. I was so relieve about that." Memories like these disquieted my grandmother; she would sit back in her chair, close her eyes and let out a long sigh, as if such times had occurred only yesterday.

"Can I help you, Mama?" my mother asked.

"*Oui*, we got to get Edward settle … and then I need to go do the milking and feed the calves," she sighed as she turned her groggy son toward the house.

"No, Mama, you don't need to milk. We did it."

"You what?"

"Yes, me and Papa, we did it … and then Ernie helped me with the separating … we didn't know when you'd be back … it's all done. I just finished cleaning the machine."

"*Merci beaucoup, ma chérie*," my grandmother's eyes shimmered with the beginnings of tears. She examined for a moment her daughter's soft, toothy smile, and then turned to look at the long, lean form of her husband waving a wide arch of farewell to George as he drove out of the yard.

He turned to her, "Well, I got to finish the chores unless you need help with the boy."

She smiled and took a deep breath, "No, Florence can help me open the chesterfield. I want Edward close if he need anything. I come out to feed the calves in a while."

The coal oil lamp shone an amber circle, casting rings of shadows in the dusk-darkened living room as they made up the bed. Edward sat motionless, eyes closed, in the rocking chair.

"The girls are already in bed, I'll sleep with them tonight, Mama," my mother said, "And Ernie's in the attic … he didn't eat much supper." Then she touched her brother's shoulder in a light caress, "Goodnight, Edward," and slipped silently into the bedroom.

My grandmother removed his boots, then his socks and helped him step out of his overalls. *"Bien,* my son," she whispered. He lay down gingerly on his back, hugging his casted arm with the other, turned his head away from the light and closed his eyes again. She would have stood watching him for a long while, waiting for a sound or movement that might indicate pain. When there was none, only the deep, even breaths of sleep, she shuffled to the bedroom and peeked through the curtain to check on the girls. She couldn't help but smile despite the overwhelming weariness that had begun to settle deep in her bones. There they were, three in a row, smallest to biggest. Three manes of blond hair that looked like one pile of golden silk; Helen closest to the wall, Eva in the middle and my mother barely on the edge of the bed, her slender arm draped over the two like the wing of a mother bird; she raised her head and whispered, "Mama?"

"Good night, *ma chérie.*"

"Good night, Mama."

My grandmother sighed and backed away from the curtain only a few steps to sit on her own bed. She took off her glasses and laid them on her lap, and covering her face, began to cry silently in the dark. Only a small hint of light flickered in from the living room. For some time she let the tears flow. And then, as if called to attention, she quickly wiped her face with the corner of her skirt and put on her glasses, folding the soft wires behind her ears next to the delicate skin, and touched the outside corners of the frames with her index fingers to settle them squarely on her face. She stopped to check on Edward and then made her way up the flight of tiny steps to the attic. To Ernie.

"Us kids were everything to Mom," my Aunt Helen tells me, "there was nothing she wouldn't do for us. We all knew it, too. Maybe she tried hard to be good to us because Dad … well, he just seemed to be in his

own little world, he'd go off into the fields or wherever he went and we
wouldn't see him all day, but Mom she was always there …"

The small, square window at the top of the roof's peak let in the
dusky light, which landed in a crumpled square on my mother's
empty bed. In its shadow, Ernie lay on his back in the bed he usually
shared with Edward, his left hand behind his head, his eyes open.

"Hi, Mama."

My grandmother leaned forward with her hands on her thighs,
bending close to look at him, and smiled, "So, you in bed early
tonight, eh?"

"*Oui.*"

"You help your sister with the separating … *merci.*"

"It weren't nothing."

"Well, I think maybe you come help me feed the calves, too?"

"I can't feed the calves like you do, Mama."

"You could. But it take patience."

"I'm no good at patience."

"No?"

"No."

My grandmother sat down on the edge of the bed and watched
him as he stared at the ceiling.

"Where's Edward? Is he … hurt bad?

"He's sleeping on the chesterfield tonight. His arm, it broke, like I
thought. Dr. Crane, he put it in a nice cast … he's all right." She
smoothed her son's hair away from his forehead and rested her hand
on his head. "Ernie, what happen today?"

"He was riding that calf and he fell off. That's all."

"Did you ride the calf, too?"

"No. I wanted to but Edward, he hogged it. He get to do everything."

"Ernie …"

"He does! He get the last slice of bread. He get to help Papa. He
get to drive the wagon …" Ernie tried to gulp away his tears. "But, but
I don't … I don't mean to do it."

"Do what?"

"It just happen."

"What happen?"

"I … I pull the tail."

"The calf's tail? You pull the calf's tail?"

"How do I know it's going to jump like that? I just wanted to stop Edward from riding more. I ... I'm sorry, Mama."

"Ernie, Ernie, Ernie." My grandmother's voice softened with each repetition. "Shh. Patience, my son. You got to learn to be patient." She sat stoically as he cried himself to sleep and then slipped away to do her chores.

"On the farm it doesn't matter what happens, good or bad, rain or shine, the chores have to be done." My mother ponders for a moment, "It was a hard life in so many ways ... kind of a simple life, a good life ... but hard. Does that make sense?"

I imagine the damp evening air being cool on her face, and my grandmother closing her eyes involuntarily, taking in the feel of it. She walked slowly, carefully, carrying the buckets of skimmed milk for the calves. As she approached the barn she could hear my grandfather singing, "When the m-moon shines over the c-c-cow shed, I'll be waiting at the k-k-kitchen door for you ..." and couldn't help but smile. He was tending to the cows, bedding their stalls with fresh straw. "Ah, there you are. I think maybe you forsake me tonight, Mama."

"No, I don't forsake the calves. They're hungry."

"And what about me?"

"Florence, she make you your dinner tonight. What else you want?"

"I want my beautiful wife to dance with me in the moonlight."

My grandfather smiled at her, his eyes glinting and twinkling like water reflecting sun, "So, we dance now, *m'amour?*"

She looked up at him and wondered how she could care so much for someone who so often made her prickle with vexation. She would have known that he was trying to charm her just as he did all those years ago with his teasing talk and slow smile. She wanted to be angry with him for Ernie's sake. But she spoke nothing of it and instead murmured, "I think I might be too tired for dancing tonight ... besides, I got to do my chores."

"Well, I help you then," he said, picking up the milk stool and opening the calves' pen for her.

"Merci," she said quietly and sat with one pail of skim milk at each of her sides. Making a soft clicking sound with her tongue, she coaxed one of the calves to her. As it approached she spoke in a low,

even tone, "That's a good girl … come on now …" and gently guided its head toward the pail while she put one hand in the milk, lifting her index and middle fingers out of the liquid to simulate a teat. My grandmother remained still while the calf sucked on her fingers, drawing milk into its mouth in the process. In this way, she would have fed the calves, one by one. And while she sat in the dimming light I expect she thought about her sons and decided that she would not share with anyone what Ernie had told her about Edward's accident. It would do no good and likely only cause more problems, as it seemed to her that my grandfather was the one who caused her sons' quarrels, mostly without intention, but sometimes with it.

The day's events would have sidled through her mind all that night and into the next morning: as she milked the cows and separated the milk; while she worked and squeezed the butter, and pressed it into molds; and as she made her bread, pouring the warm milk and yeast mixture into the hole she made in the bowl of flour. The mixture looked like a brown pond nestled in hills of snow. With the tips of her fingers she scooped small sections of the flour hills toward the yeasty pond and pressed them down in short pushes, intermittently moving the bowl clockwise with her right palm. The metal bowl scraped and clunked an iambic tune as she pushed and turned, pushed and turned, moving the dough, moving the thoughts in her mind.

"Marie-Anne."

"Oh!" Her hands flew from the dough to her cheeks. "Isaie, you scared me. Why don't you say something?"

He laughed. "I did."

She frowned and went back to work. "The butter's ready to put in the well."

My grandfather walked to the table and stood next to her.

"You hear me?" She looked up at him.

"*Oui.*" He was smiling. "But first … you got flour on your cheeks." He cupped his hands around her face and rubbed her delicate skin with his thumbs. They must have been rough and probably smelled like hay. "You tired, eh?"

"*Oui, je suis.*"

He released his embrace and slapped his hands against his sides, "Well, I go to the pasture to mend a piece of fence." Then he picked up the tub of butter and disappeared.

My grandmother watched him leave and then continued to study the door as if he was still there, an apparition, elusive, like her feelings about him. She quit kneading the dough, formed it into a large, smooth ball in the bowl and covered it with a dish towel, then set it on the corner of the warm stove to rise. She cleaned her hands in the wash basin, grabbed the empty fuel bucket from beside the stove and went outside. The fresh, morning wind played in her hair as she scanned the yard for the children, all of whom were foraging for chicken eggs. She could see the boys sitting together in the shade of the granary next to the chicken coop.

"I need more cow-pies," she called out, swinging the empty bucket in front of her. Ernie scrambled to his feet and ran to her in his awkward, bobbling gallop. He was smiling.

"What're you two doing?"

"Edward, he's a little bit tired, so I'm sitting with him. We give our eggs to Florence."

"You think his arm's hurting?'

"No, Mama. But I'll do his work if it does."

"I need to get the stove nice and hot to bake my bread. Can you get me some cow-pies?"

"*Oui*, I'll do it. Edward can watch me."

My grandmother's breath caught in her chest; she cleared her throat involuntarily and smiled at her son. She must have wanted to ask him if Edward knew what actually happened the day before. But she didn't. She let that be between them. It only mattered to her that they were together, like always.

Sixty years later, I am sitting in a café in Radville across a chrome and grey-green Arborite-topped table from my Uncle Ernie. This is the same café where he and my mother and the other kids would have sat with my grandparents on Saturday evenings after they delivered my grandmother's butter and eggs to the general store and bought groceries for the coming week. The place where my grandfather would buy my grandmother a dish of vanilla ice cream – two rounded scoops in a small, stemmed, glass dish with a fluted edge – and Jersey Milk chocolate bars for the kids. The café was the farming community's gathering place where neighbours, who rarely saw one another except on weekend trips to town, came to socialize. During the week, everyone was far too busy with the labour of the land. Only the winter months afforded farmers any leisure time to meet, usually in each others' homes, for evenings of food, drink and games of whist or canasta.

Dr. Crane has long since retired, but the place where he practiced, a block east of Radville's wide and dusty main street, is still referred to as the doctor's house. Signs printed with family names like Larsen or Bourassa, familiar to me from the stories of neighbouring farmers, hang over the doors of the three blocks of businesses that make up the town's core. A few of the buildings retain false fronts and remind me of the old, Western movie sets; others have been refurbished with coats of white paint, their tenants, no doubt, turned over several times since the nineteen thirties. But the old three-storey Radville Hotel, the original Canadian Imperial Bank of Commerce and the café remain just as they were, a repeating dream, an ever-present memory for the elders of the community and a touch point of history for those of us once or twice removed from the stories those buildings hold.

"Yeah, I pulled that calf's tail," Uncle Ernie says, "Course, I don't know it would jump like that." His eyes twinkle behind wire-rimmed glasses as he quirks a left-sided grin.

I giggle, which pleases him, and his face breaks into a full-on smile. His eyes are as blue as my mother's, my grandmother's, too. They match the sky-colour of the checks in his plaid, cotton shirt. A white baseball cap perches on his head, cocked slightly back and to the right, jaunty and casual, the way farmers, for some unknown reason, always seem to don their hats.

My uncle tells me a lot that day. He tells me things I expect he's never told anyone but his wife, Betty, because he is a quiet man, reserved and, at seventy-nine years old, still shy, I think; still very much aware of his physical disability that got translated into a mental one. But he is anything but that.

"You know, the ol' man won't let me have any part of the farm. He always thought I wasn't worth nothing to it because of this bum arm and leg of mine. Edward, he got the whole thing."

I am stunned. Ernie, the first-born and due the inheritance of the farm. My mother, who is with us, gasps; in all these years she did not know this. In her generation, daughters got married off; family business remained with the sons.

"But you worked the farm with Uncle Edward after Gramma and Grampa left?"

"Yeah, sure I did but I didn't get nothing for it ... enough to live on ... but not the land."

"Did Gramma agree with this?

"She couldn't tell the ol' man nothing when it come to that. He was stubborn as a mule. So, Mom, she just try to keep peace in the family. I guess maybe we all just try to keep the peace."

We – Ernie, Betty, my mother and I – all are silent with our own thoughts. I wonder what my Uncle Edward would have said about this, gone now for many years. I remember him as a gentle, kind man, not one to take anything that wasn't his, least of all from his brother. And, I think of all the stories I know of my grandmother's life, of her determination, her business acumen, her ability to carry a myriad of tasks and complete them all, her unrelenting care for her children, and yet this one thing, this very important thing, she could not accomplish. She could not convince my grandfather, my seemingly carefree, jovial grandfather to give Ernie his rightful due. And I know my grandmother well enough to understand that this would have grieved her deeply and remained a constant rumble in her mind.

"Well," Ernie breaks the silence, his words reassuringly matter-of-fact, "that's the way it was ... It's okay. It took me some time, but I saved some money, and then I went out and bought my own farm."

My Uncle Ernie and Aunt Betty farmed successfully just outside of Radville for some forty years until, having no children to take over the land, they sold it and moved to Weyburn, twenty miles away.

After lunch at the café, we take a drive to my grandparents' old farm, now run by my Uncle Edward's family, then to the Fradette farms – all of my grandmother's brothers' land, including my great grandparents' place. The original house built with wood transported by train from Quebec still stands, unoccupied now and used only for storage of farm supplies. Our last stop: Uncle Ernie's old farm.

"I wish I'd sold just the land and kept the farmyard. It would have kept me busy, just working in the yard ... and we would still have a garden ... but with this bum arm and leg of mine I started to worry I might take a fall." He stares out the car window toward the tree-bordered yard with its white bungalow house. Bright multicoloured bands of annuals line the front walk, the lawn a lush, minty green. "We kept the garden back there in the corner," he says quietly, as if remembering at this very moment the tilling of its black earth in preparation for planting. "I sure loved this place. It's not the same when you live in town, but ..." he looks over at me from the passenger seat, his eyes rimmed with tears, and smiles his crooked smile, "Well, you know, sometimes that's just the way she goes."

RHUBARB COBBLER

3–4 cups chopped rhubarb tossed with1/2 cup sugar, or other fruit*	1 cup cream
	1 1/2 teaspoon baking powder
	A touch of salt
1/2 cup sugar	
1 egg, beaten	

Put prepared fruit in a 9 inch baking pan to fill approximately 3/4 full (fruit will cook down). Mix remaining ingredients and pour over fruit. Bake in a preheated 375 degree oven for approximately 30 minutes or until golden brown. Serve hot or cold with heavy cream, whipped cream or ice cream.

* If using apples, toss with 3 tablespoons sugar
  If using peaches or berries, toss with 2 tablespoons of sugar

My grandmother made the most of everything from her garden – canning, stewing, pickling – but also picking and eating fresh each day.

GREEN TOMATO KETCHUP

2 dozen green tomatoes	1 cup white sugar
1 dozen medium onions	3 tablespoons pickling spices,
Pickling salt	wrapped in cheesecloth
White vinegar	

In a large stockpot put one layer of thinly sliced tomatoes followed by one layer of thinly sliced onions. Sprinkle with pickling salt and repeat layering tomatoes, onions and salt. Let stand overnight.

Drain liquid from the pot and rinse contents. Drain again, then add enough vinegar to cover the tomato-onion mixture. Add sugar and pickling spices. Cook slowly on low heat for 2–3 hours, stirring often to make sure the bottom doesn't burn. Put in canning jars and seal.

Please note: As food safety and knowledge has improved over the decades, so has knowledge of the dangers of preserving, such as the risk of botulism. If attempting this recipe, please first consult a reputable source for safety guidelines such as Health Canada.

Sometimes called "Chowchow" this tomato ketchup is the only canning recipe my grandmother used for tomatoes. She preferred to eat the rest of her crop, sun-ripened and red, straight out of the garden. Throughout the rest of the year, if she needed tomatoes – mostly to make tomato soup – she bought them by the can at Jack Seede's store.

TOMATO SOUP

3 tablespoons butter
1 medium onion
1 large can of tomatoes
1 teaspoon baking soda
2 cups milk

Melt butter in a saucepan on the stove. Add thinly sliced onions and cook for a few minutes until transparent. Add tomatoes and baking soda, stirring constantly. Add milk gradually, stirring constantly. Heat just to boiling point, then reduce temperature and simmer for approximately 5 minutes. Serve.

The key to this recipe is adding the baking soda, which keeps the milk – added very slowly with much stirring – from curdling. How did my grandmother know such things?

PICKLES

Cucumbers   Water
Dillweed   1 cup salt
Vinegar

Wash cucumbers. Put fresh dillweed in the bottom of a stone crock (with a cover that snaps on) and top with cucumbers. Make a solution of 1 part vinegar, 3 parts water mixed with 1 cup of salt (enough solution to cover cucumbers) and bring to a boil. Pour over cucumbers, cover and store for 1 month in a cool place. If a scum forms on the top, spoon it off and use pickles as soon as possible.

This is the way my grandmother made pickles, not in sealers that lasted through the winter but fresh and crunchy. Forget about the scum.

POTATO SALAD DRESSING

4 eggs, beaten	1/2 teaspoon yellow mustard
1/2 cup vinegar	1/2 cup sugar
1 cup milk	1/2 teaspoon each, salt and pepper

Mix all ingredients in a pot on the stove. Cook at medium heat to a slow boil, until slightly thickened. Cool. Toss with cooked potatoes.

Leftover dressing could be kept in a jar tightly sealed in the cold cellar for several days. But my grandmother usually used it quickly, planning several meals that included big bowls of potato salad, which included some chopped spring onions, sliced radishes and some leaf lettuce torn into bits ... all fresh from her garden, of course. Today a batch of this dressing could keep for about three weeks in a refrigerator.

SALMON LOAF

1 can salmon
1 egg, separated
1 cup bread crumbs
Salt and pepper, to taste
1/2 cup milk

Beat egg yolk. Mix together salmon, bread crumbs, milk, salt and pepper with the beaten yolk. Beat the egg white separately and gently add in to the salmon mixture. Pour into a small loaf pan. Cook in a preheated 350 degree oven for 1 hour until nice and brown.

When the scarcity of the Depression years passed and she could afford to buy a few more supplies from the general store, my grandmother often made salmon loaf on Fridays or during Lent instead of mashed potato pie or omelettes and, no doubt, used the crusty ends of bread loaves to make the crumbs.

BREAD

Milk	3 packages dry yeast
2 heaping tablespoons lard	2 tablespoons sugar
2 teaspoons sugar	Flour
5 teaspoons salt	Cold water
Warm water	

In a small cooking pot on the stove pour in one knuckle of milk and add lard, salt and 2 teaspoons of sugar. Heat until lard just melts.

In the meantime, into a small bowl put about 1 cup warm water. Add 2 tablespoons of sugar and the yeast. Stir gently and let mixture sit until it just starts to bubble.

Put 1 1/2 inches of flour around the inside of the basin of a large bread-mixing bowl. Pour a little cold water into the milk mixture to make it lukewarm. Pour this into the basin of the bread-mixing bowl. Add 1 small cooking pot of warm water into the basin; then add yeast mixture. Gently stir the liquid with your fingers.

Fold the flour into the liquid with an open hand. Gradually add 3 to 4 cups of flour to the basin until you need to use both hands for mixing. Roll the mixture from the sides of the bowl into the centre of the dough and punch it down. Continue until the dough begins to crumble slightly in the rolls. Remove excess flour from the bowl.

Make dough into a nice big ball, cover and set in a warm place for 2 hours. Roll and punch the dough again. Cover and let sit for 1 hour.

Grease hands and cut off pieces of dough, molding it into elongated rounds. Put in greased loaf pans. Cover and let rise until doubled in size.

Bake in preheated 410 degree oven for 45 minutes. Remove from pans and brush tops of loaves with a little butter.

The instructions of this recipe were handed down from my grandmother to my mother, and then from my mother to me. I watched my mother make a batch of bread, just as she watched her mother, and we wrote down what we observed. Of course a knuckle of milk, which is up to the first joint of my pointer finger, and a small pot, the smallest I have in my collection of four, are completely subjective. But so is bread making. If the three of us were together and followed the same instructions at the same time and put our bread in the same oven, still the baked loaves would have different looks, textures and tastes, formed from our own unique ways of preparing and kneading the dough. May this recipe help you find your own way, too. But bread making is an art, so you might have to be patient.

Do you remember that?

"Your grampa, he make a chicken catcher. He use an old broom handle and put a loop of wire on the end. He'd corner the chicken and catch his legs in that wire and then grab it by the head and swing the neck around real fast so it broke off … but," she adds, leaning forward in her chair, "you got to be real strong to kill a chicken like that so it won't suffer. Only mens do it that way. Me, I chop the head off with a certainty axe I used to have just for butchering chickens." She shrugs her shoulders and puckers her lips, "Well, that how we do it in those days."

I can hear my grandmother say it just that way, matter-of-factly, without worry about the death of the chicken but at the same time, humane. My mother speaks about her childhood and her own years as a farm woman in a different way.

"She kept that little axe in the corner of the shanty, right next to the door." I'm certain she's not aware of it, but when my mother tells me this, her voice is small and reverent, like a child's. "It was real sharp and none of us kids were allowed to touch it. We knew we were having fried chicken for dinner when she got it out …"

That little axe held a terrible and awesome power clutched in my grandmother's hand. She was a petite woman, but I expect she looked large and fierce in her ankle-length housedress and long white apron as she marched out to the coop, the axe, a menacing glint in the sun.

"She knew which chickens to butcher, too … you know, the ones that weren't laying anymore."

My grandmother had a way with chickens, just like she had a way with cows. And her expertise helped to keep her family fed in the lean years. If she wasn't gathering eggs to sell in town, she gathered them to put under the hens that loved to sit. She knew which were the good nesters and kept them in a small shed, dark and warm, where they clucked and sat on a dozen or more eggs, which she had slipped under their downy bellies, until the chicks hatched. She raised chickens, she knew one from the other and she killed them. It was the way you lived off the land.

"She would get a chicken with that catcher and pin its open wings on the chopping block with her knee. Then she stretched the neck out with one hand and made one big, fast chop with the axe. That's it. She let go of it and that chicken's body would run around for a little bit and then just fall over ..." my mother shakes her head, "seems awful, thinking about it now, but that's how I killed chickens, too ... do you remember that?"

I say I remember, but I feel far away from the scene, not next to my mother in the crook of her arm as I usually was. Instead I'm huddled next to the shed with my fingers in my mouth, hesitantly shifting my eyes away from staring at my brown, oxford shoes and the knot in one of the laces, toward her and the axe, and the chickens. But I vividly remember the chicken heads afterwards. Once, our old, black dog swallowed two of them whole and then vomited them back up into the dirt, their red, head combs dripping in yellow bile. These I examined in disgust and wonder, imagining them once again on the feathered bodies, pecking at the ground and clucking their soft, absent-minded chatter.

My memories of those early years of my life on the farm are isolated, but utterly clear. I recall the dusty beams of sunlight that tried to peek through the cracks in the wood plank walls of the chicken coop. There was the thick smell of hay mixed with chicken shit, and my mother's slow, stealthy hand reaching under the hens in search of their warm eggs. I remember holding my breath as I walked by them, my arms glued to my sides. I would do nothing to disturb those regal birds whose fierce, protective pecks could break a child's delicate skin.

Or, the last rays of the sun low in the sky, pushing up behind the barn and turning its red lines and curves into a silhouette of solid black; my mother's crackling soprano call, "Coboss, coboss." She would be leaning against the fence, one hand on her hip, waiting for the cattle to lumber in from the pasture; her bare legs, the full skirt of her dress billowing just slightly in the hint of a breeze. And then, in the barn: the stainless steel cones of the milking machine that covered a cow's teats. They have replaced the soft, hard pulls of my mother's hands, the hum and clunk of the machine instead of her gentle, "Whoa there, girl," calming the nervous Holstein.

In many ways I lived like an only child on the farm, being the youngest of five children. My two sisters and then two brothers, five and seven years older than me, were all in school by the time I wanted and needed companionship. Except for Sunday family gatherings, there wasn't much of that; the closest neighbours lived several miles down the road. When I wasn't toddling after my mother as she did her chores, I was alone playing tea party with my dolls, making pretend meals on that old coal stove in the yard, or sitting in my little rocking chair "reading" a stack of books – bedtime stories I had memorized. But looking back now, maybe those solitary times were in some way necessary, part of my preparation for the days I now spend alone creating and imagining, reading and writing.

My parents kept an immaculate farmyard. When you drove into it, our modest, white house stood to the right in front of a big grass lawn and had a huge garden behind it. The machine shed, granaries, chicken coop and barn were all to the left, painted red with white trim. The entire yard was bordered with thousands of pines and poplar trees my parents had planted themselves many years prior. In my memory they towered and were thick like a forest. At one edge of that forest, in the shade of those tall, tall trees, my brothers built an intricate, miniature farm. They fashioned a barn from locking plastic bricks, constructed a fence made of toothpicks and Popsicle sticks and had tiny, farm animals grazing and pecking in just the right spots. My favourite part of their design was a well made out of a tin can dug into the dirt so that it ran flush to the ground. A frame above the well held a small plastic bucket on a string that could be lowered to gather a thimble of water. How I wanted to draw from that well, but I was not allowed to touch anything in their farmyard. I could only watch them play from a distance six paces back from that most wonderful, miniature world.

They had a clubhouse, too. It was small, not more than eight feet square, painted bright yellow with a wooden latch inside the door to keep non-members out. Of course, the non-member was me. I would stand outside that little house and try to hear what the two of them were talking about as wisps of smoke curled out of the cracks in the walls, the result of one of their not-so-secret ceremonies: puffing on old cigarette butts hoarded from the farmyard, discarded here and there by my father and visiting neighbours. I was a girl and too young to be part of their play except once that I remember; one clear moment of inclusion in which I was allowed to accompany them, but only if I swore to secrecy, "Cross my heart and hope to die," my chubby fingers making the motion over my chest as I repeated the words.

The boys had somehow secured pieces of a salt block, which my father set out for the cows to lick. I had not witnessed this clandestine venture, so I can only imagine them sneaking out to the pasture like soldiers, crouching, then sidling on their bellies in the tall grass, a hammer and chisel clutched in their grubby hands. They giggle and snicker as they use their weapons to break the big, blue square apart, stuff their shirts with the booty and crawl their way back to the machine shed where they hide the pieces in the tool shed in the recesses of a drawer caked with oil and dirt.

On that particular day, once they were sure that my father was nowhere near, my older brother instructed us to sneak, one by one, out to the shed where he retrieved three pieces of salt. We huddled there on the dirt floor furiously licking the blue chunks. My heart thumped in my chest. I was afraid of being caught but thrilled to be included in my brothers' covert fun. I closed my eyes and continued to lick. Then suddenly, without warning, my salt was ripped from my hands. "That's enough," one of them whispered. The blue chunks went back in their hiding place and the three of us walked, as nonchalantly as children could, out of the dank shed into the brilliance of a cloudless, prairie afternoon. My tongue felt raw and tingly. I wanted to ask my brothers if theirs felt the same, but I had sworn never to speak of our doings. Besides, they were already halfway to the clubhouse, their feet kicking up little puffs of dust with their long-legged strides.

When I am away from the land as I knew it as a child, I long for the thick freshness of the air after a thunderstorm, the lavender seas of flax fields rolling in the breeze, and the nutty, grassy scent of ripening wheat. I think of popping peas in my sister's garden, nibbling the sweet, green orbs from the pods while stepping carefully, one foot in front of the other, between the rows on my way to the raspberry patch. I want to hear the caw of giant, black crows, the trilling melody of the meadowlark or the sound of poplar leaves rustling in the wind. All of this to restore my memories of the land to the full, vivid richness they deserve and I desire.

As it turned out, my grandmother and I both became travellers of a sort, out of a certain kind of restlessness, moving here and there, away from our prairie homes. I think in our own ways we traded the known for the unknown just as our relative, Jean Fradet, did when he set out for New France generations ago. But I wonder if my grandmother remembered her days on the prairies as fondly as I do now, or would she have looked back and seen only long years of hardship? I suppose a bit of both. The difficulties of her day-to-day reality could never be forgotten, but I know her heart pumped with blood that loved the land and all that it meant to be near it. Such genetics always possess a person. Of this, I am quite sure.

FRIED CHICKEN

1 frying chicken, cut into pieces
3 tablespoons of butter (approximately)
1/2 cup of flour
Salt and pepper, to taste

Skin the chicken and soak in cold water. Brown the butter in a Dutch oven (an iron pot works best) at medium high heat. In the meantime, drain the chicken and pat dry. Put all the pieces in the pot and brown on both sides. Sprinkle flour over the top of the meat and add salt and pepper.

Cook slowly at medium to medium-low heat, stirring pieces often, until meat looks nice and brown and a bit crispy. Serve.

The juice of the slow-cooked chicken, which mixes with the butter and flour and turns into crunchy little morsels that attach themselves to the fall-off-the bone meat, defines this dish and always, always makes you want more. Give thanks to the chicken for its sacrifice and enjoy.

That keep me busy enough

In the mid-nineteen forties my grandparents passed on the care of the farm to my uncles and moved to Radville so my aunts could attend Catholic school. It was a noble reason to make such a move, but I'm sure neither of them had the least inkling of how hard their separation from the land would be, or what a serpentine path their lives would take upon leaving it. Maybe that's why, during their first years of living in town, my grandmother insisted on returning to the farm every day to make lunch and dinner for Ernie and Edward.

She would have stood at the window in the early hours of morning looking out to the empty Radville street, waiting for one of her sons to pick her up and take her to the old farmhouse. Her hands clasped together at her waist as if priming to sing a song and, at her feet, bags of fresh vegetables from the garden, meat for cooking and an array of baked goods – the supplies she would need for the meals that day. I wonder if, as she stood there, she felt the same anticipation and excitement as I do when I leave the close quarters of my urban life to return to the prairie? Did she long to see its golden fields rippling as if the wind had fingers stroking the ripe heads of wheat in long gentle sweeps, and the clouds, puffing in tall cones across the unending expanse of blue? Or did she spend those quiet moments thinking back over the years that she and my grandfather harvested the land together?

In the days of early fall, when they still lived on the farm, my grandmother took meals out to my grandfather and teenaged uncles in the field. Next to her in the horse and buggy she would have the black, iron pot heaped with fried chicken along with a big bowl of potato salad. And, no doubt, there would be a rhubarb or peach pie – or maybe both, baked that morning in the dim light of dawn – nestled in kitchen towels on the floor of the buggy next to a jug of milk and kettle of coffee. As she drove, she would search the horizon: from afar the three of them looked like a stand of brush; as she got closer, a slow moving herd of cows; until finally, she could see their forms – her husband's and sons' – like pencil lines in their leanness near the curved bulk of the team of horses, moving methodically. By the time she reached them, they would have stopped working and would be waiting for her, hats in hand and wiping their brows on their sleeves, their faces tan, foreheads white.

If she remembered such times as she waited at the window in Radville, did they make her long for the deep scent of ripened wheat, a mixture of musk and dust, grass and hay – unforgettable and distinctly soothing. Did she dream of letting the sun settle on her face and rest in the familiar glow, just as I do when I think about being near the land? Maybe she only remembered the bustle of that season, when she not only served meals but worked the harvest as well.

My mother tells me she wore my grandfather's overalls, the bottoms rolled several times into loose cuffs, and a pair of his work-boots made wearable by donning two pairs of heavy, grey wool socks; she looked just a little like a clown but, of course, her purpose was serious. After feeding the men, she would stay on to work in the field. While my grandfather drove the binder, she – side by side with her sons – stacked the sheaves, bending and gathering in a rhythm that could only come from the deep, physical memory of repetition.

I think that if my grandmother were here with me now she would tell me that she would have been happier in her life had she stayed on the farm. She would say of her sons, "Let them look after the land," and wave her arm in the air as if shooing a couple of flies from her face. "Just give me a cow or two and some chickens and my garden. I'm very happy with that. That keep me busy enough." But the needs of the family always came first and that initial move to Radville was only one of many that spanned three provinces and at least thirty different homes or apartments.

As I look back on my grandparents' lives, I can see that many of these moves centred on the desire to be helpful to their children or the need to be near them. Others reflected their constant financial concerns, and for my grandmother, alone in her later years, several came out of a deep, uncomfortable restlessness. She was a woman who knew nothing but a busy, productive life. Initially she may have been glad to be free of the overwhelming work of the farm, but she also was accustomed to its hardships and rewards. After she left the farm, my grandmother was known for saying, "I'm so depress," and maybe this happened when she didn't have enough to occupy her time or her mind. Maybe the act of moving, the bustle of packing and resettling, energized and comforted her in some way.

It was only a few years until my grandparents left Radville for Regina, where my Aunt Eva had moved to work but also where she found herself lonely and longing for her family. Instead of insisting that their daughter return home, they went to her and started a boarding house funded by my grandfather's sister, Louise, and her husband, Joe. My grandmother enjoyed the flurry of activity that came with running the place, but issues arose that eventually ended the business.

They were having trouble making any profit because she was too generous. In the course of a week my grandmother never cooked the same meal twice, and instead of portioning plates of food for the boarders, as was the custom and which would have kept down the cost, she served everything family-style, as she would have in her own home. Her boarders – eight healthy, and very hungry, young men – often ate two or three helpings of food at every meal. Instead of cooking less, she cooked more to keep up with their appetites.

"Those guys just loved living with Mom. She treated them like they were her own sons … she even packed them lunches to take to work! Boarding houses didn't do that in those days," my Aunt Helen recalls, "but Mom did."

In the end, the frenetic pace of continual meal preparation and service – all without the benefit of food refrigeration – as well as the ongoing demands of doing the laundry, housecleaning and yard-work took their toll on my grandmother as she approached her mid-fifties. Even though my grandfather helped her, the venture could not be maintained without her.

"You know, she started to have some female troubles and with all that work at the boarding house, it just got to be too much. She didn't want to quit it, she had to."

If my grandparents had put their own wants in front of every-thing else then, I believe they would have moved to the lower mainland of British Columbia. They loved "the coast," as they called it, a popular winter destination among farmers from the central provinces. From the late forties when they left the farm to the early sixties, my grandparents visited there whenever they could afford to. Sometimes they rented an apartment for a few months, but most often stayed with Audelie and Henri in a small upstairs room of their house in New Westminster. My great-aunt and great-uncle left their farm around the same time my grandparents first moved to Radville. One of their sons took over the land, and they moved to the coast where they lived out the rest of their lives.

New Westminster is one of a cluster of suburban cities situated around the mouth of the Fraser River and Vancouver's downtown core. Winters there are damp but moderate in temperature and clearly different from the foreboding cold of the snowy, prairie plains. Spring is breathtaking – magnolia trees and rhododendrons with buds the size of oranges, pinkish-white blossoms cluster like huge dollops of whipped cream in the cherry trees that line street after street of houses, their lawns like plush carpets edged with profusions of bedding plants bursting into geranium reds, pansy purples and snapdragon yellows. In the summer, when the sun shines and the clouds stay out at sea, the moist elixir of heat and ocean breeze draws everyone outside to sit and read, or walk and behold the days' perfection.

My grandparents might have dreamed of moving to British Columbia after they closed the boarding house and finding a modest home of their own where they would have kept a big garden in a yard bordered with my grandmother's favourite flowers. Her many doilies would have dotted the furniture and my grandfather's violin would have been propped in the corner of the living room, ready to be played with the least bit of coaxing. And they would have had enough years there together to find a new rhythm to their lives, one that included card games and dances at the seniors' centre. But that opportunity was lost before such a dream could take shape in their minds. Instead they bought a tiny house on McTavish Street in Regina to remain close to Eva, who by then was married to a volatile, difficult man and had two small boys.

My Aunt Helen, who still lived with my grandparents at that time, recalls, "It wasn't much of a house but Mom scrubbed it clean and made new curtains for all the windows. Of course, she kept a garden in the back, and Dad, he dug a bit of a cold cellar under the house. We still had no fridge then, so Mom needed someplace to keep her baking and food that needed to be kept cool ... she helped Eva a lot then, looking after the boys while she went to work. Sometimes, when things got really bad for Eva, she and the little guys just stayed there with us. Those times were pretty hard on Mom."

Everyone who knew her will tell you that my grandmother was a woman of many moods. She could be jovial, generous with her laughter and very talkative. At other times she was sullen, prone to bouts of tears; these were the times she would complain about being "depress." I wonder if, after leaving the farm, she missed the clear and rhythmic purpose of life on the land and that this caused her deep distress. But back then, she couldn't, or maybe wouldn't, articulate to anyone the source of her black moods.

"Mom seemed to be the happiest when she was in BC ... but, you know, I think she enjoyed living in that little house on McTavish, especially when she got that job," Aunt Helen tells me. "She sure liked that job."

For about a year and a half, my grandfather looked after the little boys while my grandmother worked with Eva at a business, the true nature of which she never quite knew. She didn't care either. With only a third grade education, she was just happy to have a job, a delightful purpose for getting up in the morning when she would bustle around her house in the early hours doing all the chores she could have taken the entire day to do had she not been working. Then she would slip out of her housecoat into nylon stockings, secured by the little balls and hooks of a garter belt; a full slip, lacy on the breast and hem; and, I imagine, a blue, cotton dress – one that cinches at the waist with a patent leather belt, three-quarter length sleeves and a shirt collar that she would unfold at the back of the neck to perk up the style. And because my grandmother always accessorized her carefully coordinated outfits, I expect there would be jewellery: maybe a string of fake pearls and button earrings to match, or a simple cameo brooch on the left side of her chest. A dusting of powder on her face, rouge on her cheeks, a sweep of red on her lips, and she was off to work, early by ten minutes or so, to spend the day stuffing envelopes and licking stamps.

"Oh yes, I like that job," she told me, "You know, it get me out of the house. I meet some people ... we have nice talks ... it pass the time for me."

My grandmother was not a smoker but she smoked when she had that job.

"Well," she explained matter-of-factly, "we go for our coffee break and everybody have a cigarette with their coffee, so I have one, too."

I picture her sitting in the café, accompanied by my aunt and three or four other women from her office, legs crossed at the knee, her full skirt hanging in folds, almost touching the linoleum tiled floor. Her left arm folded across her waist, holding her right arm, hand pointed to the ceiling, delicately cradling the cigarette between her index and middle fingers. She'd put the filter to her lips, suck and then blow out in the same fluid movement, leaving a little cloud of smoke to dissipate in the flow of her laughter.

My grandmother smoked, but according to my mother, she said she never inhaled. Maybe it was the act of smoking that intrigued her, made her feel like a modern woman.

"She was so happy to make some of her own money," my aunt laughed, a half-giggle, half-guffaw, infectious, shoulders shaking a little, just like my grandmother. "The first thing she bought was a refrigerator and a suit for Dad … then she got a new television and some furniture … and then she got herself a fur coat. Oh, she was so proud of that coat."

I seem to remember a photograph of my grandmother standing on the porch step of the little, yellow house on McTavish Street; ridges of snow pose on the windowsills as demurely as she posed for the photograph, one arm crooked, holding the straps of her black purse, and the other, with gloved hand, rested on her thigh, indenting the mink fur ever so slightly. I think that job opened a window to a different world for my grandmother and gave her a new vision of herself, at least for a time.

But one day, without notice, the business closed its doors. Some say the owners were on the run after the authorities caught on to what was only referred to as shady activities. Soon thereafter, my grandparents rented out the house and moved to my childhood home, Brandon, Manitoba, a farm community hub. The city was a quiet place with tree-lined streets and yards with big vegetable gardens and flowerbeds filled with petunias and alyssum; a leafy dome set in the midst of miles and miles of farmland. They moved this time because my grandfather got full-time employment setting up farm machinery in my father's implement business.

By then my grandmother was on her way to becoming an expert packer, wrapping and bending to load the cardboard boxes as she once bent to the sheaves in the wheat fields. In the trunks that she and my grandfather had brought into their marriage holding all their worldly possessions – hers, square in wood-trimmed leather; his, humpbacked, copper-studded and of blue metal – she packed her special things, held securely by layers of dishcloths and linens. A tightly fitted jigsaw puzzle she learned to do with her eyes closed. On the farm her trunk sat next to their bed, used as a nightstand or fashioned into a baby crib, and otherwise stored clothes and items she wanted close at hand. My grandfather's stayed locked in the corner of the attic. It mostly contained things she no longer needed but could not part with. My mother tells me that in a drawer that fit snuggly into a ledge that bordered the top part of the trunk's interior my grandmother kept some photos, along with a few newspaper clippings and a small, red leather-bound notebook.

I have that book now, on loan from my mother's safekeeping. In tentative, open French script, at one end of it my grandmother recorded the births of her five children, starting with the first, and written like this:

Pére
Isaie Lacaille
Mére,
Marie-Anne Lacaille
Elle est nie
Marie Flourange
Rita Lacaille
est venu au monde
le 14 Septembre 1923
a la éte Batiser le 16 Sep
Parin Ferdinand
Fradette

Maraine
Philoméne Fradette
nié a Radville, Sask.
Bautiser Curie Kigener

And at the other end of the book, she recorded the deaths of her and my grandfather's parents, with the final entry being her husband's passing:

La mort de
Isaie Lacaille

il est mort le
5 de Aout 1965
a l'age de 66 ans

A été enterré a
Radville, Sask.
August 10 - 1965

In that red book, all the pages in between the five births on one end and the five deaths on the other are blank pages that I wish now held some record of her life. Instead, I study a pile of photographs and draw from my own memories of her and the memories of others who knew her in order to shape the life of this woman who was too busy, or not busy enough, to record events except for the highest moments of joy and the lowest of sorrow.

My mother tells me the brown-edged portrait of the young man from Deleau, Manitoba, was among the photos she also kept in that drawer of my grandfather's trunk. But it has disappeared. I wonder how or why, because I know that it and the relationship it represented were important to my grandmother. And it is confounding to me that she never kept his letters or my grandfather's, written to her from the British Columbia mines. Maybe she destroyed them to keep their contents private. But it could be that sentimentality deferred to practicality – there were just so many things one could continue to pack and move. My grandmother would never have been without her black, iron cooking pot or her bread-making bowl or the small yellow one she used to mix pie crust dough. Her kitchenware, a few wall plaques, some ceramic figurines and her doilies followed her everywhere, and because of them, no matter where she lived, each place became distinctly hers.

A couple years before she died, my grandmother started giving away some of the items she had been so careful to keep with her over the years. The pink crystal salt and pepper shakers went to my Aunt Helen, her Wearever cooking pots to Aunt Eva, some opalescent glass candy dishes to my mother and one Christmas she sent me her ceramic puppy. Amidst the abundance of gifts my husband and sons always heap upon me, I screeched and moaned and wept deeply over this old, brown and tan dog of indistinct breed, sitting lazily on his haunches, about eight inches tall, eyes and chipped ears cocked up to the right, and his black nose and whiskered muzzle splotchy white where the paint had worn off. But he represented my grandmother. I always knew where to find him when I visited her – sitting on a doily, on the floor, next to the ceramic kitten, in front of the television stand.

I don't know what happened to her ceramic kitten. Maybe it accidentally got broken or lost, just as the photo and old letters may have, in the shuffle of her many moves. If my grandmother were here today I would ask her.

But when she and my grandfather moved to Brandon from Regina, all of these special things, packed solidly and neatly, were still with her. And as always, my grandmother adapted to her new home, the adjustment made easier by being close to my mother and our family. Though, I expect she missed her job as her world in Brandon was very small: living in an odd, little apartment in a big red house on Sixth Street; keeping a garden in the yard they shared with other tenants. Her days were spent walking the three blocks to the Co-op store for her groceries, and on Sundays, going to Mass and having family dinners that ended in long evenings of canasta with my parents. There wasn't much else for her then, except unknowingly to give me some of my most memorable times with her as a child.

I spent many afternoons visiting and sometimes stayed overnight at my grandparents' home when my parents went out for the evening or away for a weekend. Everything about being there was magical to me. The old house stood four storeys high including the attic and seemed like a castle compared to the one-storey bungalows that lined my neighbourhood's streets. My grandparents lived in the rooms at the back of the house, which had a small, square kitchen with one tall window that let in the light of the warm western sun in the afternoons. In the dark and musty parlour, my grandfather sometimes played his violin while I sat cross-legged under the Singer sewing machine, on its foot pump, rocking back and forth to the music. And I loved climbing the narrow staircase to its second-storey bedroom, the linoleum floor warped and cracked and nailed into place, but the ceiling peaked high like a dollhouse. The room always smelled like a bouquet of summer flowers. To me, this was their kingdom and I was their honoured guest.

When I drive past this house now, it and the yard look normal in size. But back then, everything seemed so huge. The yard stretched deep and wide, the maple, oak and poplar trees that shaded it towered majestically. Great stands of caragana, lilac and gooseberry bushes hugged the sides of the house. I remember helping my grandmother pick the greenish-white berries to make jam, her fingers plucking and then gently laying the fruit in a plastic ice cream pail. I tried to copy her rhythm. Then she popped one in her mouth and smiled at me. "Try one," she said. And so I did; the taste so bitter my eyes teared and my throat squeezed shut. "Gooseberries, they're my favourite," she said as she chewed and continued picking. That she could tolerate the sourness amazes me even now. I've never eaten a gooseberry since.

In the large garden in the back corner of the yard, my grandmother grew lettuce, radishes, green onions, carrots, potatoes, tomatoes and always a trellis of sweet peas, just as she did on the farm. In the cool of summer afternoons, before she went out to tend its black earth or pick vegetables for the evening meal, she always made me a special snack. On the old, wood picnic table just outside the door of the apartment, she would set out a glass of cold, chocolate milk and two store-bought Sultana biscuits on a plate, even though she always had a batch of homemade oatmeal cookies on hand. I can't recall why she would not have given me those except that she considered store-bought baking a treat. Next to them, a colouring book and crayons and some storybooks – things to keep me occupied while she worked. But mostly I just sat, swinging my legs back and forth, sipping the buttery chocolate and nibbling the crumbly biscuit to find a raisin, and watched my grandmother hoe and bend, the pleats of her housedress swishing with her movement. The sun shining through the leaves of those tall trees dappling her with light, the breeze pungent with the honey scent of sweet peas.

And I remember, too, sitting in her tiny, square kitchen – my grandmother, my mother and I. One day, in particular, the sun shone through the open window leaving a shimmering parallelogram of light on the small table. The sheer curtains puffed, only slightly, in a gentle push of wind. I took a bite of crumbly, sweet matrimonial cake, a sip of chocolate milk from a small, etched crystal glass and lay down on a wooden chair with my head in my mother's lap, so that I could see her face upside down. I watched her mouth move as she spoke. Her tongue looked like it was flapping and her large top teeth, now her bottom teeth, looked extraordinarily strange. I changed positions to watch my grandmother talk upside down. When she laughed, her lips made long, tight lines along the tops of her teeth. I closed my eyes. Maybe I fell asleep. When I opened them again my grandmother had a cigarette in her upside down lips and her eyes squinted in little, half-moon smiles behind her glasses. She was saying to my mother, "Just suck on it and then blow it right out. You don't need to take in the smoke."

JOHNNYCAKE

1 egg
1 teaspoon baking soda
1/2 cup sugar
1 pinch of salt

1 tablespoon butter
1 cup flour or 1 tasse
 de fleur de blé d'Inde
1 cup milk

Mix ingredients in order given. Pour into a 9 inch lightly greased baking pan. Bake in a preheated 350 degree oven for 20 to 25 minutes, or until firm. Cool and cut into serving squares.

My grandfather used the expression "fleur de blé d'Inde" to describe cornmeal. He loved johnnycake as much as he loved his mother's chocolate pie; it is the only dish he ever cooked on his own. During the time my grandmother and Aunt Eva worked together in that shady little business office, he often made it for himself and his young grandsons.

BANANA LOAF

3/4 cup white sugar
1/4 cup shortening
3 bananas, mashed
1 egg

1 teaspoon baking soda
1 1/2 cups flour
Pinch of salt
Chopped walnuts, if desired

Mix sugar and shortening. Add bananas and egg. Mix dry ingredients together and then fold into wet mixture. Add walnuts. Put mixture into a lightly greased loaf pan and bake in a preheated 375 degree oven for 45 to 50 minutes.

From the winter evenings on the farm, playing whist with friends, to Sunday nights in Brandon, playing canasta with my parents, banana loaf and nut bread were always two of my grandmother's favourites to serve after a rousing game of cards.

NUT BREAD

1 cup sugar	2 cups milk
4 cups flour	1 egg
4 teaspoons salt	
1 cup chopped walnuts	

Combine dry ingredients. In a separate bowl, beat milk and egg together. Mix the two together and let sit for 1/2 hour in a warm place. Bake in a loaf pan in a preheated 325 degree oven for 1 hour.

MATRIMONIAL CAKE

1 pound dates	2 cups rolled oats
1 cup brown sugar	1 3/4 cups flour
Water	1 cup butter, melted

Chop dates and cook with a 1/2 cup of the brown sugar and just enough water to cover until mushy and easy to spread. Cool slightly.

Combine balance of ingredients to a crumbly texture. Put half of this mixture in the bottom of a 9 inch square pan and pat down firmly. Spread with cooked dates. Add remaining oat mixture. Bake in a preheated 375 degree oven for 45 minutes. Cool before serving.

With a cup of tea or coffee in the kitchen in the afternoon; after dinner, usually accompanied by a selection of her cookies; and often, later in the evening concluding a long session of gin rummy or canasta, buttery, melt-in-your-mouth matrimonial cake was always a welcome treat.

GINGER COOKIES

1 cup white sugar
2 eggs
1 cup molasses
1 teaspoon butter

1 tablespoon baking soda
2 tablespoons vinegar
2 cups flour
2 tablespoons ginger

Combine sugar, eggs, molasses and butter. Mix well. Dissolve baking soda in vinegar and add to mixture. Add flour and ginger to make dough.

On a floured surface, roll out dough to 1/4 inch thick and cut into rounds with a cookie cutter.

Place rounds on a lightly greased cookie sheet and bake in a preheated 350 degree oven for 8 to 10 minutes. Cool slightly before removing from cookie sheet.

These ginger cookies come out of the oven very crisp and are especially good dunked in a cold glass of milk. But be careful, it's impossible to have only one ... or two.

COCONUT MACAROONS

1 cup white sugar
3 tablespoons cold water
1 egg white, beaten

1 pinch salt
3 cups coconut
1 teaspoon vanilla

Boil sugar and water until it threads. Pour over beaten egg white and beat well. Add vanilla, salt and coconut.

Drop by spoonful on a greased cookie sheet. Bake in a preheated 325 degree oven for 20 to 25 minutes until golden brown. Cool before removing from cookie sheet.

Along with her ever-present oatmeal cookies, my grandmother's ginger cookies and macaroons always held a place on her table. She would gently push the plate towards you and say, "Have another one, dear."

I don't make
no fuss

If my grandmother were alive today I know she would tell me everything. No pieces of stories would be kept secret or left untold. Today I would have made sure we remained close despite living two thousand miles from each other, in different countries, in different time zones, because I value now what I did not know then. When I was younger I was too taken up with my own life to embrace the richness and wisdom of hers.

Years ago, when I was single and she was widowed, we lived twenty minutes from each other's front door in British Columbia's lower mainland: she, in New Westminster; I, in downtown Vancouver. If you asked me back then if I followed my grandmother there I would have said no, that instead I, an enthusiastic twenty-year-old, moved there one February with the desire to explore life away from my family and away from the winter's dune-like snowdrifts. But now I think she carried more influence than I gave her credit for. I remember, as a child, the welcoming picture she painted of "the coast" after she and my grandfather returned from their visits there. "It so nice in BC, you can walk everywhere you want to go; you don't need to worry about snow; everything is always nice and green," she would say with quiet longing.

This has always been part of the glory of living in the lower mainland; the weather is made for walkers. Snow rarely falls on the city streets in its mild winters, reserved instead for the mountain range that rises eastward. However, it does rain a lot from October until April, that drizzly London-type rain, but if you have an umbrella you can still walk. That's what my grandmother did every season of the year when she moved there in the early 1970s after my grandfather died, walked – to the grocery store, the Woodward's department store, her sister Audelie's house or to Century House, the senior's centre where she played cards and attended dances – from her third-storey walk-up apartment. Of course she didn't own a car because she never had a driver's licence. My grandmother adapted, as she always did, to life as it presented itself.

From the stories my grandmother told me when I was small, I had imagined "the coast" to be a mystical, evergreen wonderland, and I wrote in a primary school essay that when I grew up I wanted to live there. Maybe this childhood vision drew me to BC, and then knowing that my grandmother would be there, I mustered the courage to step into the urban world. I always felt safe when I was near her, felt a quiet come over me. I think this was because wherever my grandmother lived she had a special way of making it feel like home, rooted and rich with her own history – our family history – and everything was always orderly and immaculately clean.

A faint, lemony scent of Mr. Clean or furniture polish inevitably lingered in the air, accompanied by a squirt of flowery air freshener and just a hint of mothballs. During the day she rarely closed window curtains, preferring the long beams of warm sunlight to brighten her rooms. She loved flowers, real and artificial. In the years that she kept a garden, or knew someone who did, a fresh bouquet graced her dining table, even if only a drinking glass of lilacs, pansies or her beloved sweet peas. The work of her busy hands was everywhere: doilies as headrests and on the arms of the sofa and chairs; doilies on the coffee table, framing ornaments and dishes of hard candy and chewy mints; doilies on the floor acting like little mats for her ceramic animals and vases of bright, plastic flowers – yellow tulips and red roses; braided rag rugs in the kitchen and at her front door. And usually when you walked in that front door a whisper of old-time country music, maybe Merle Haggard or Ray Price, tinkled out of the hi-fi console, which she would immediately turn off so she could give her full attention to you. This is how I remember our times together in BC.

And our lives were oddly similar: the loneliness of making dinner for one; watching a comedy on television with your own laughter for company; the edge of discomfort – not quite feeling safe – when you turn out the lights and lay listening to the unknown sounds of night. We both sifted through the chaff of first dates with men whom she would have met at the senior centre's dances or bridge games, and I, at work or nightclubs. The fifty-three years that separated our ages could have been fifty-three minutes.

"Come to my place and have some supper with me. It won't be nothing," she would say on the phone. And I could imagine her lips puckering, her shoulders shrugging as she says these words because that was always her way of making light of something.

"Are you sure, Gramma? We could go out to eat," I'd say.

"No, no. It's no trouble. I don't make no fuss."

And then, there she would be, smiling, "Hello, dear," with one hand on the doorknob and the other stretched out to hold my cheek and draw me in for a kiss on the lips. She smells sweet, like rose water. I am only five-foot-four but I bend to hug her soft, warm body, that lovely warmth that makes you want to hold on just a touch longer. In her early seventies, she kept her hair short, blondish-brown and curled in a light perm that haloed her head – she would be in her nineties before she stopped colouring it. She laughs as she smiles and her eyes light up in an electric twinkle just as her husband's used to do. For a moment I miss my grandfather and wonder if she does, too, after a decade of living alone.

"Come in. Come in," she says and turns toward the living room, leaving me to close the door. She shuffles not because it's the way she walks but because she has on backless slippers, the furry, fluffy kind and powder blue, the colour matching exactly the ruffle and ties of the apron she wears. I follow her but pause by the archway to her tiny kitchen. A fresh lemon pie graces the counter, its crown of meringue two inches high and glistening gold. Several pots sit on the stove, one of them black iron, in which she always cooks meat. This time: fried chicken. I know because the aroma is divinely familiar.

She has turned off the stereo and is sitting in her easy chair, her back straight, ankles crossed and hands folded in her lap, waiting for me to sit down and visit with her. There is little preparation left to do for dinner. She has already pulled out two of the Naugahyde swivel chairs from the wood-grain Arborite table now covered in a white embroidered tablecloth, and in front of each, table settings with a cup and saucer next to them for the hot tea we will have with our pie. Pink crystal salt and pepper shakers sit surrounded by a plate of sliced tomatoes; a bowl of sliced, white onions in vinegar and water; and two dishes, one piled high with dill pickles, the other with radishes. Though she bought all of these at the grocery store they will taste, as they always do, like they have been freshly picked from her garden.

This has long been a curiosity to me and everyone in my family. We would often ask one another, "Why are Gramma's tomatoes so juicy? Why do her sliced onions taste so mild and sweet?" as if on a quest for the answer to one of the mysteries of the universe. I think now that her success in these things came from her long years of weeding, hoeing, touching leaves and poking her finger around the base of root vegetables to check their sizes. Her sense was keen and developed so that even in a grocery store she could pick the best produce by sight and feel – tomatoes, the right red of ripeness, the best press of firmness. Maybe she could tell a good onion by the look and thickness of its skin, or radishes by the leafiness of their tops. If you asked her about this, she would just laugh, pleased with the sideways compliment being given to her.

I sit back on the sofa with my hand resting on its arm, feeling the rough yet delicate pattern of the doily beneath my touch.

"The weather's not been so good, eh?" She always starts the conversation with the weather, a custom of her generation and maybe also because, as is her nature, she is a bit shy to approach more intimate subjects at first. But by the time we have finished dinner – after I've shamelessly sucked several chicken bones dry; eaten a mound of her fluffy, boiled potatoes and a heap of melt-in-your-mouth cooked carrots (two more curiosities); savoured the leaf lettuce tossed in a bit of sour cream and vinegar; and sampled or cleaned up every vegetable condiment on the table – we are sipping black tea between tart-smooth mouthfuls of undeniably the best lemon meringue pie ever created and talking about the deeper things in our lives.

"Are you still seeing Joe?" I ask her.

"Yes," she pauses and looks toward the floor.

"Do you think you might marry him, Gramma?" I ask. "Wouldn't it be nice to not be alone?" But maybe I am questioning my own singleness, my own loneliness, rather than hers.

"No." Her answer is definitive. "I don't want to look after no more mens. Your grampa, that was enough for me."

I smile at her, but before I have time to comment she continues.

"Sure I get lonely sometime," she says, puckering and shrugging, "but Joe, he take me to those dances, you know. And on Fridays we play cards. Sometimes we have a meal together. That's enough." With this she waves her hand dismissively in the air.

When I married, the camaraderie of our singleness melted away. Though we still spent time together our meetings were fewer and, in the midst of my new life, I often neglected to call her for our weekly telephone conversations. We were supposed to take turns but she was just shy enough (or maybe stubborn enough) not to call me if I missed mine. But when we did talk, she was never shy about putting me in my place.

"How come you don't call me?"

"I'm sorry, Gramma, the week's just flown by with ..."

"Well, I'm all alone ... sometime that make me so depress." And this would be followed by complete silence, my clue to talk about my week so she could voice her discontent by not responding.

After a while I would say something like, "You had lots of stuff going on this week, too, didn't you, Gramma?"

Then she would start to warm up to me, little by little, with a murmur, "Mmm ..."

"Don't you play cribbage on Tuesdays?"

"Mmm ..."

"Or is it bridge on Tuesdays and cribbage on Fridays?"

"Mmm ..."

"Did you beat the pants off that stinky guy in cribbage this week?"

My grandmother was very particular about her hygiene and appearance, always dressing smartly with matching earrings and necklace, or sometimes pinning a vibrantly coloured scarf around her neck with a brooch, and wearing a light coat of lipstick and her subtle, flowery perfume. It was not unlike her to comment on people's unkempt appearances or smells after she had met them, like the old fellow she sometimes played cards with at the centre, "He always wear the same damn shirt ... but he's a widower, you know ... he got nobody to tell him how bad he smell."

When she and my grandfather lived on the farm with their five children, even in the bone dry years of the thirties' summer droughts or the deep cold of prairie winters, my grandmother made sure that everyone had a bath on Saturday afternoon before their weekly trip to town. They used a metal tub, dragged in from the shanty, set next to the wood stove in the kitchen, where my grandmother heated buckets of warm water for the bath over the still-hot flame from her morning baking. They took turns by age, the youngest going first, which was disconcerting to my mother, the oldest; she shudders at the memory of it now.

"Mom bathed Helen and Eva first ... in the smallest amount of water. Then after she got them dried, she added another bucket for Edward and Ernie. Those two long-legged boys squeezed into the tub together, their knees hugged up close to their chests."

One brother's toes on top of the other's, my grandmother scrubbed one back while the other one washed his own face and body; then they would switch, while she directed them to clean every crease and crevice with the foamy bar of soap she purchased from the Rawleigh's travelling salesman. When they were done, she added one more bucket of warm water.

"Then it was my turn. I hated getting in that tub after the boys. They were always so dirty ..." my mother wiggles with discomfort, then laughs and shakes her head, "but then Mom still got in there after me ... and poor, old Dad had to bathe last ... in that same water. Can you imagine? But with no indoor plumbing that's how you had to do it. Anyway, we got the dirt washed off and everybody smelled nice and clean. That's what Mom liked." My mother sits for a moment, her arms folded across her chest, her thumb rubbing the crook of her arm, a remnant habit of busy hands. "She made sure we got our hair washed once a week, too ... but not on Saturday. Saturdays were always too busy ... she usually baked all morning, and then with getting the butter and cream ready to take to town, and all us kids dressed ..." she stares somberly at the floor, "honestly, sometimes I don't know how she did it all ... but, anyway ..." she sighs and looks up, her eyes watery and bright, just like my grand-mother's. "Mom liked to use the nice, soft water from the rain barrel to wash our hair. We bent over the wash bin in the kitchen and she'd rub our scalps so hard her whole body shook and we had to hang on to the table for dear life. But, boy, it felt good and our hair was so clean it squeaked."

No, in her later years as a widow, my grandmother would never have dated a man whose hair was dirty or clothes, scruffy, and certainly no one with body odour. She might even shy away from having a simple conversation with such a person. She had very clear ideas about men, even as a young woman. "Your grampa, he look very good when I first meet him. He keep his hair nice and he wear nice clothes to that party. I don't pay no attention to the guy other-wise." She chuckled when she told me this, but I knew she meant it.

I also knew that my mention of beating a stinky guy at cribbage would amuse her and so I used this kind of ploy when our telephone conversations became stilted. I knew that if I could get her to laugh about anything, the silent treatment would be over and then we'd find our way into a lovely conversation, which would always end with her saying something like, "Well dear, it was so nice for you to call. I sure enjoy our talks."

I enjoyed those talks, too. They often led to my grandmother's recollections of her life. Sometimes she offered them up as a service to me. From her years on the farm, I might learn how to make pressed chicken; find out when to pick tomatoes from the vine, or what it's like to have that first baby in your life. But mostly she recalled events as if for their own sake, a way of keeping the past alive; her past, which was so much bigger and fuller than her pres-ent. Still, I didn't listen to her stories then as I would now.

Youth carries with it a type of tunnel vision, a self-centred imme-diacy. At least that's the way it seems to me as I look back on that time when I was in the midst of fashioning myself into a modern woman who could do it all, a member of that generation of females reaching for liberation but still tied to the homemaking traditions of the 1950s. I had married a corporate pilot, worked as a bookkeeper and focused on things like deciding what colour to paint the hallway to best match the wallpaper in the kitchen. I didn't make the connec-tion to my grandmother once being a young woman like myself; a woman who ran her own cottage industry selling her home-churned butter and eggs at the general store every week. A woman who, while raising five children, worked in the fields with her husband like a hired man; and who wallpapered the attic with layers of newspapers and flour glue to make it look nice and keep out the dust and rain. While I made macramé plant holders to hang in the sunlight of my living room's big picture window, I didn't realize that she had spent long evenings, well past everyone else's bedtime, braiding rags cut from old clothes into beautifully patterned rugs to lay over her cold, wood floors. So much of her life was born out of necessity.

I wish I'd known, during our talks, that twenty-five years later I would be compelled to write about my grandmother's life, which spanned the twentieth century and reflected the experiences of many prairie women of that time. Their way of life modelled grace and ingenuity in the midst of tremendous hardship and can still inform us about being female in this world today. In my youth and early adulthood, the times I was closest to my grandmother, I didn't know to ask the questions I have now, or I didn't have the courage to press past her private nature to get her to talk about the things she seemed reluctant to share and which now, years after her death, I would give anything to know. If she were with me today, I'd make her laugh to break her silence, just as I used to, and then she would tell me everything. And I would know how to listen.

RAW ONIONS

1 large white or Spanish onion
Cold water
1 tablespoon vinegar
Salt and pepper, to taste

Peel onion and cut into 1/4 inch slices. Put in a bowl, add salt and pepper and just cover slices with cold water. Add vinegar and let marinade for approximately 1/2 hour before serving.

Of course, finding the perfect onion, mild and juicy, makes this simple dish spectacular. But even if you are not as adept at perfect picking as my grandmother was, the vinegar and water marinade does wonders for any regular old onion.

LEMON MERINGUE PIE

3 heaping tablespoons cornstarch   2 tablespoons cold water
1/4 cup water   3 cups boiling water
2 lemons, juiced   2 tablespoons butter
1 1/2 cups sugar   1 baked 9 inch pie shell
4 eggs, separated

Mix cornstarch with 1/4 cup of water to make a smooth paste.

Mix the juice of the two lemons with one cup of sugar, the egg yolks and cold water in a saucepan on stove at medium heat. Add boiling water and cornstarch paste, stirring constantly. Add butter and continue to stir for approximately 3 to 4 minutes until sauce is smooth and thickened. Cool slightly and pour into pie shell.

To make meringue, beat egg whites with remaining 1/2 cup of sugar until fluffy. Spread over lemon filling and bake in preheated 375 degree oven until top is just golden brown.

In her later years, when my grandmother made dessert, it was sure to be lemon pie, mostly because she knew if she asked you what you'd like her to make, the answer would always be, "Lemon pie, please, Gramma!" The recipe is here on the page and I have made it but never managed to replicate the tart and creamy smoothness of her filling, nor, of course, the mile-high meringue.

I just want to hurry up

One summer day while I was living in Vancouver, and my mother and oldest sister, Elaine, were visiting, the three of us planned to have dinner that evening with my grandmother after she finished her afternoon of card-playing at the Century House senior centre. I can't remember now what we were doing that day except, for some reason, we were all dressed smartly: skirts and blouses, nylons and sandals. In the late seventies everyone still wore nylons, even in the summer. Maybe we'd gone for lunch at one of the downtown restaurants that looked out over Vancouver Harbour, but more likely we'd gone shopping, as we would have wanted to save our appetites for Gramma's cooking.

But I do remember that we arrived at her apartment early and decided to walk the half-mile or so to the senior centre to surprise her. We strolled the broad sidewalk, three in a row, admiring yards of straight flower beds and manicured cedars, and others that were wildly planted with rhododendrons branching like jungle trees, and making bets on what my grandmother would serve for dinner. We put our money on her family-famous fried chicken, but hoped that she might make skinny steak this time.

I don't know if my grandmother invented skinny steak, but she started making it back in the 1920s when each fall she and my grandfather would butcher a cow for winter food. They put the various cuts of meat, including roasts, in gunny sacks and froze them in the granary, nestled amidst the cold wheat or barley. Skinny steak came from a frozen roast, cut with a very sharp knife into carpaccio-thin slices and fried in butter. Practically speaking, this sounds to me like a rather creative response to serving a last minute meal, but maybe it was one of my grandmother's ways of doling out meat in smaller servings to make it last through the winter. In any case, it became such a family favourite that she continued to serve beef this way long after she left the farm, purchasing a roast at the Safeway store and then freezing it for the sole purpose of making her skinny steak: heaping platefuls of sizzling, fragrant curls of beef drizzled with buttery juice from the frying pan.

Smiling in the warmth of the perfect summer sun, we moved on to the discussion of dessert: would she make lemon meringue pie or angel food cake? I know it sounds like we were inordinately preoccupied by food, but when it came to my grandmother's cooking this always happened.

"She still whips meringue by hand … with an egg beater, you know," my mother said proudly.

"No!"

"Really?"

My sister and I could hardly imagine such a thing, being from the burgeoning electronic age.

"Uh huh, and the egg whites for her angel food cake, too … it's harder to do now because the eggs aren't as fresh, but that's her way, so that's how she keeps doing it. Of course, on the farm she used eggs straight from the coop. Oh, those eggs made such a beautiful cake … seemed like a foot high," she said, raising her hand in an expressive measurement. "And, if she made an angel food cake, she always made a couple of spice cakes along with it to use up the egg yolks. She was never short of energy or ideas, that woman."

As we approached Century House, the sun receded behind the tall pine trees that surrounded the building. Inside, the reception area was empty, but a rumbling chatter echoed from an open door to the left. Like three little girls, we giggled and peeked in to look for my grandmother, whom we saw sitting at a table at the far end of the room. She said something and laid down her cards; her laughter, so familiar to our ears, seemed to ring above the others. She must have had a good hand.

We pulled back from the door, not wanting her to see us. Soon a few folks started to wander from the room. We decided to wait for her to come out to make it a bigger surprise, but five minutes later she still hadn't appeared. Impatient, I decided to go find her, only to discover from one of her playing partners that she had already gone, having left the building from the rear exit.

"That's okay," I said to my mother and sister, "We'll catch up to her. The guy said we just missed her."

We scurried down the street, the same way we came, the direct and only way we knew she would walk to and from Century House, sure that we would see her, one arm crooked at her side holding her purse, the other swinging rhythmically with her stride. But we didn't. We walked at a clipped pace – our brows glistening – and didn't speak except to mumble, "Where the heck is she?" but we could not spot her. Even in her later years my grandmother was a powerful walker, her strides longer and steadier than you would expect from a small woman, barely five feet tall; determined strides that seemed to reflect her once busy life. I suppose a person doesn't let go of such determined busyness. It must stay in the body's memory even if the mind tries to let go.

We arrived at her apartment building puffing and bewildered, and feeling not so smartly dressed, as all of us were now sweating profusely.

"I just don't know where she could have gotten to," my mother said.

We stood at the entrance catching our breaths and looking for her up the street we had just furiously marched down.

"You don't suppose she's already home?" my sister offered.

"Well," my mother shrugged, "I don't think so … but I guess we could go check."

We trudged up the three flights of stairs and stumbled toward her door at the end of the hall. A familiar aroma floated in the air. We looked at one another – silly, stupefied looks. I knocked on the door.

My grandmother opened it wearing her fluffy bedroom slippers and a frilly apron around her waist. She looked like she always did when she was waiting for me to come to dinner – no flushed cheeks, no glistening brow.

"Oh, you're here! It so good to see you," she reached up and held my cheek, guiding my face to hers for a kiss on the lips. She smelled rosewater sweet; not the least bit sweaty. "Come in, come in," she said. I shuffled past her so she could greet my mother and sister in the same way, and poked my head into the kitchen. Skinny steak crackled in the frying pan on the stove; next to it, a substantial pile of thinly sliced beef waited ready to fry. And nestled in the corner of the counter, every bit of a foot high and covered in the soft white peaks of icing, my grandmother's glorious angel food cake. And then, I wondered where the spice cakes might be hiding.

"Mom, we went to Century House to surprise you," my mother stated incredulously.

"You did?"

"Gramma, how the heck did you get home so fast?"

"I don't know," she shrugged her shoulders and puckered her lips, "I just want to hurry up and get home to start my skinny steak before you get here."

SKINNY STEAK

1 frozen chuck or round roast
Butter, as needed
Salt and pepper, to taste

Take meat out of granary or freezer a couple of hours prior to using. When ready to prepare the meal, melt a nice pad of butter in a heavy iron frying pan. With a sharp carving knife, shave very thin slices of meat from the only slightly thawed roast and put in the hot pan. Be sure not to overlap pieces. Fry on both sides, adding salt and pepper as desired. Put cooked slices on a plate in a warm oven. Add more butter to the frying pan as needed and continue frying until the desired amount of meat is cooked. Add a little water to the empty pan, scrape the bottom and pour juice over meat. Serve.

You can rewrap the remaining frozen roast for more skinny steak meals or continue to thaw in the refrigerator and cook as a pot roast the next day.

In the spring, before the remaining frozen beef in the granary could begin to thaw, my grandmother sliced the meat into thin steaks, fried it up and put it in a stone crock covered with a layer of suet (beef fat), which she stored in the cellar. She called it canned steak and served it by heating the slices in a cast iron pan.

"It wasn't as delicious as skinny steak," my mother tells me, "but it still tasted darn good."

ANGEL FOOD CAKE

1 cup sifted cake flour	1/4 teaspoon salt
3/4 cup sugar	3/4 cup sugar
12 egg whites	1 1/2 teaspoons vanilla
1 1/2 teaspoons cream of tartar	

Sift flour with first 3/4 cup of sugar four times. Beat egg whites with cream of tartar and salt until stiff enough to form soft peaks but still moist and glossy. Add remaining sugar, two tablespoons at a time, and the vanilla, continuing to beat vigorously until the meringue holds into stiff peaks. Next, sift about 1/4 of the flour mixture over the whites and gently fold in, then fold in the remaining flour in fourths.

Carefully put batter in an ungreased 10 inch tube pan and bake in a 375 degree preheated oven for 35 to 40 minutes, or until done. Invert pan on a baking rack and let cool.

Almost always, my grandmother used sweet, marshmallowy "seven minute icing" on her angel food cake. After all, what are a few more minutes of beating egg whites when you've spent twenty at the kitchen counter whipping twelve of them by hand for a cake?

SEVEN MINUTE ICING

2 unbeaten egg whites	Dash of salt
1/3 cup cold water	1/4 teaspoon cream of tartar
1 1/2 cups of sugar	1 teaspoon vanilla

Put water in bottom pot of a double boiler, place on stove and turn on high heat to bring to a boil. Place all ingredients, except vanilla, in top pot of a double boiler (off the stove) and beat (with egg beater or electric mixer) for 1 minute to blend.

Place pot over bottom pot when water begins to boil and cook, beating constantly, until the frosting forms stiff peaks (approximately 7 minutes, but be sure not to overcook).

Remove top pot from boiling water, add vanilla and beat about two minutes, until the mixture is of spreading consistency. It is now ready to ice the cake.

In the summer, when eggs were plentiful, my grandmother whipped up (literally) an angel food cake almost every Saturday morning as well as a selection of other baked goods, which she stored and used for desserts throughout the week. The following recipes recount what you could be sure to find on the root cellar shelves along with rows and rows of Mason jars packed with garden vegetables, meat and jams.

SPICE CAKE

6 egg yolks (or 1 whole egg)	1/2 teaspoon salt
1/2 cup shortening, melted	3/4 teaspoon allspice
1 cup sugar	3/4 teaspoon cinnamon
1 cup buttermilk or sour milk	1/2 teaspoon cloves
1 1/2 cups flour	1/4 teaspoon nutmeg
1 tablespoon baking soda	1/2 cup raisins

Mix eggs, shortening and sugar. Add buttermilk and stir. Fold in all dry ingredients. Pour into a lightly greased 9 inch square pan and bake in a preheated 375 degree oven for 25 minutes.

Cool and top with icing of choice.

My grandmother's spice cake was one of my grandfather's favourites. She made it week after week, no doubt to please him but also to use up the egg yolks left over from the angel food cake. Sometimes she'd make a white cake instead, or one of each. But, my mother tells me, when she used yolks to make white cake, they turned the "white" to yellow.

WHITE CAKE

6 egg yolks (or 1 whole egg)	1 teaspoon vanilla
1 cup sugar	2 cups flour
1/2 cup shortening	3 teaspoons baking powder
2/3 cup milk	1/2 teaspoon salt

Beat egg(s) and combine with sugar and shortening. Add milk and vanilla. Mix in dry ingredients. Pour into a lightly greased 9 inch square pan and bake in a preheated 375 degree oven for 30 minutes until golden brown.

Cool and top with icing of choice.

Now, of course, no one ever ate a cake in my grandmother's house without some sort of frosting on it, so she had a lovely, little selection of quick toppings she could make in a few minutes, just before serving.

CAKE ICING

1 cup icing sugar
Heavy cream
1 tablespoon cocoa (optional)

Mix the icing sugar with enough cream to make the mixture smooth and easy to spread. Add the cocoa for chocolate icing.

GRAMMA'S STICKY ICING

7 tablespoons milk
1 tablespoon cocoa
7 tablespoons sugar
1/4 teaspoon vanilla
1 tablespoon butter

Mix all ingredients together in a pan on top of the stove. Cook at medium to medium-high heat, stirring constantly until the sauce forms a string from the lifted spoon. Cool slightly.

My grandmother served sticky icing on every kind of cake she baked, at one time or another. I remember eating this sweet, gooey concoction right off the spoon. As my mother says, "Use your imagination; it tastes good on everything!"

DREAM CAKE

White part:

1 cup flour
1/2 cup butter
1 tablespoon white sugar

Mix all ingredients to make a crumbly consistency. Put into a 9 inch square pan and pat down firmly. Bake in a preheated 325 degree oven for 10 minutes. Cool slightly.

Brown part:

2 eggs	1 teaspoon baking powder
1 cup brown sugar	1/2 cup nuts
1 tablespoon flour	1/2 cup coconut

Mix all ingredients and spread over the white part of the cake. Bake at 325 degrees for approximately 25 to 30 minutes, or until golden brown. Cool and slice.

While living on the farm my grandmother made this cake every week just as she did the angel food cake. It was easy to slip the "white part" in the oven between other items and finish off the "brown part" at the end of the morning's baking. She not only enjoyed making dream cake, she liked eating it, too.

I been here long enough

I did not attend my grandmother's funeral in March of 2000. Ironically, when she died I was closer to her in miles than I had been in many years and in the place she loved – British Columbia – attending my father-in-law's funeral, giving the eulogy for a man I deeply admired. My mother was not there either. She was on the other side of the world at my sister Elaine's home in Dubai, UAE, and had been there only twenty-four hours when she got the news.

Even though she was ninety-seven, my grandmother left us more quickly than we were ready for. I remember my mother's voice on the telephone. I remember my own. Both strained with emotion and confusion. Wanting to be there but confined by our circumstances. After talking with her siblings, my mother advised them to proceed with the funeral. She said her farewell in her own way. Every day she walked among the dark, flowing robes of Muslim women to a small Catholic church where she prayed and lit red votive candles in remembrance of her mother.

I had my last visit with my grandmother in her tiny apartment in a seniors' complex in downtown Regina. It was as small as, or smaller than, many of the places in which she had made her home from the time she was a child in Saint-Lazare de Bellechasse. Still, when I walked in her door, this one was as all of them ever were – with a pullout sofa in the living room for overnight guests, its hard angles softened by lacy doilies draped on the arms and back, an easy chair that rocked and a coffee table precisely set with special knick-knacks and little dishes of hard candy and peppermints.

If I remember correctly she still had in that little apartment the same old hi-fi console with a television, record player and radio. In the course of many moves my grandmother had left the records behind, but she had taken to watching a few "shows" in the after-noon, and then the CBC News at six o'clock, so she could keep abreast of the weather and political events, both of which she liked to talk about. Otherwise, country music from a local radio station tinkled softly from the glittery black speakers. Several oranges sat brightly in a bowl on the counter in the kitchenette, from which she would hand-squeeze the juice each morning for breakfast. A loaf of bread, no longer homemade, tucked in a plastic bag and twist-tied just so, waited to be sliced, toasted and slathered with Cheez Whiz. I remember her bathroom being decorated in pink – a fluffy pink bath mat and toilet seat cover, a pink bar of soap, pink artificial flowers on the vanity. The scent of floral air spray lingered, wafting across the tiny hall to her bedroom; a floral spread on her bed, the dresser set with a hand mirror and comb as if inserted there from another time. A time long ago.

Some days she would go for a walk in the nearby Victoria Park or do a little shopping with my widowed Aunt Eva, who also lived alone just a few miles away in the northern part of the city. She kept to herself in those last years, except for visits with family members. She could have gone downstairs to the complex's common room to play cards, even take her meals there. But she refused. Instead, she would make a small batch of grand-père et grand-mère or fried chicken in gravy, the way her mother, Philomène, used to make it, and eat from that for several days. And if she didn't feel like cooking, well, there was always toast and Cheez Whiz. The kitchen was too small to make meals as she once did, so when company came she liked to go out. The Diplomat was her favourite restaurant, and the wait staff knew her by name.

"Good evening, Mrs. Lacaille. So nice to see you again."

Her response was always the same and, now as I reflect upon it, embodied everything I know my grandmother to be – she would nod her greeting with a shy smile, but looked like the Queen, the handles of her purse strapped over one crooked arm, as she walked to her usual table and then waited demurely for the waiter to pull back her chair. She would sit, legs crossed at the ankles and hands in her lap, eyes lowered toward her place setting until he offered the menu, which she knew by heart.

But most often, then in her mid-nineties, my grandmother spent many hours of each day in her easy chair, rocking back and forth to the music, eyes closed, rosary in hand.

"I just sit here and remember all those times in my life. Sometime they make me laugh, sometime, well, I cry," she said. "You know, I live a long time. I don't know why God don't take me now. I been here long enough." The days of milking cows and churning butter, weeding the garden or stooking wheat – the physical work that helped quiet her mind – were gone. Now, only the soft push of one foot against the floor and the roll of rosary beads between fingers served to keep her peace.

I wonder if, as she rocked, my grandmother laughed or cried when she considered the serpentine journey of her life, how she and my grandfather lived a little like gypsies camping out in one place or another after they left the farm and that, of their many moves over the years, she often lived as a guest in other people's homes. I've thought of it, of how difficult it must have been for a woman of her own mind and sensibilities to have to submit to the lifestyle of others – first as a young bride in the elder Lacailles' home. Then when the family left the farm for Radville, she, my aunts and grandfather lived with his brother Raymond. Raymond, who was unmarried and eccentric in his ways, the baby of the family and spoiled by Soufrine. While in his home, my grandmother took over where Soufrine left off because she felt beholden to him for providing her family with a place to live. She kept the house pristinely clean, did his laundry and catered to his peculiar eating habits. He refused to eat dairy products of any kind, used pork fat instead of butter, ate his morning oatmeal covered in sugar, but without milk. So she cooked separate meals or patiently prepared a special plate for him without the offensive items.

They left Raymond's home in Radville to live in British Columbia for a few of the harsh winter months during those years, and made arrangements for the girls to do their schoolwork by correspondence. However, because they could not afford to rent a place, even then they lived under someone else's roof – first, with my grandmother's older sister Marilda – in a single room with a hot plate for cooking. And there were problems: Marilda liked to cook lamb, and my grandfather hated lamb.

"Your grampa, he always complain that my sister's house stink like mutton. He grumble and say, 'We stink like mutton all winter.'"

My grandmother laughs a little at this recollection, but I think it must have been very hard for her in those close quarters; and I wonder how much of the mild BC winter she actually enjoyed.

Consequently, they were Marilda's guests only once. On other trips they stayed with Audelie and Henri. My grandmother cooked most of the meals, as Audelie didn't have much flair in the kitchen, and I expect she kept the house spotless as payment for their stay.

Even the move to Regina to be near Eva involved others. I'm told that those plans came about one night during a visit with my grandfather's sister Louise and her husband, Joe. It is unclear whose idea it was exactly, but it likely began as a jovial conversation after a game of canasta. As always, my grandmother would have laid out a handsome spread of food – tender roast beef sandwiches on freshly baked bread slathered with butter; homemade dill pickles; matrimonial cake and oatmeal cookies – the usual assortment she had on hand. And as they patted their full stomachs and sipped hot coffee, I imagine Joe saying, "You're the best cook I know, Marie-Anne. *Oui,* the very best."

Such adulation would not have bothered Louise because she was not a good cook, nor did she care that she was not a good cook.

Being shy, my grandmother probably blushed, not sure how to accept Joe's compliment.

And then, because I am familiar with my grandfather's nature, I'm sure it was he who said, "Eh, Joe, you have lots of money. Buy a big house and we'll come to live with you and my Marie-Anne, she'll cook for you all day long. And we could have boarders. Make lots of money, eh?"

And so, Joe bought that big, three-storey house in central Regina. He and Louise lived in a large room on the third floor. My grandparents and aunts lived in the basement; though my uncles, Edward and Ernie, joined them as well during the winter months when there was less to do on the farm. And, of course, they took in those eight boarders, all working, young men.

Joe must have enjoyed the living arrangement. He had never been fed so well in all of his married life because Louise, like her brother Raymond, had a number of food idiosyncrasies, which she insisted on living by. She had a penchant for eating only raw vegetables such as carrots or cabbage, and those only one at a time; she would make a meal of only carrots. If she cooked, which of course she didn't when she and Joe lived in that big house in Regina, it was one item, for example, a chicken. And there it was – chicken on a plate, no potatoes, no carrots, just chicken. But her favourite food was garlic. Raw garlic popped in her mouth one clove at a time like pieces of candy.

The boarders began to complain about the pungent odour wafting down from the third floor. It permeated their clothing; it was in their nostrils when they awoke in the morning. I can only imagine the whispering discourse between my grandparents.

"You got to tell Louise to stop eating that damn garlic. Everybody's going to move out if you don't."

"You tell her how bad it stink in here. She's your sister."

"Maybe we should tell Joe. You think Joe knows how bad it stink?"

"I don't know. Maybe he's used to it."

"Sacremogee! The man, he sleep with that stink, too."

I suspect that it was my grandmother who talked to Joe about the garlic. They had formed a deep friendship over the years, one in which a delicate matter such as this could be discussed without offence or insult. Louise did cut back on the garlic and, of course, the boarders remained. My grandmother would have remembered that time with some amusement and, possibly, some regret. "Those young guys begged Mom to keep the boarding house going," my mother tells me. "She was so good to them ... and fed them so well. They all got fat while they stayed with her!"

Finally, in the winter of 1967, after having lived under all those relatives' roofs, then in the house on McTavish in Regina, the little apartment in Brandon and after having rented several dingy places – small rooms they could afford for a few months during the winter – near Audelie and Henri but not underfoot, my grandparents finally decided to settle in British Columbia for good. With the money they got from the sale of the Regina property, they made an offer on a house in New Westminster.

"Oh, Mom was so excited about that little house. It was a dream come true for her." My mother's voice fades into a whisper as she speaks these words.

Before the deal was finalized my grandfather died suddenly from a massive stroke. He was sixty-five years old. My grandmother's dream blew away like a dandelion puff in a gust of prairie wind, her partner of forty-four years, gone, and she was without a home, once again. She boarded a train and took her husband's body back to

Saskatchewan to be buried next to his parents, Louis and Soufrine, in the Radville cemetery.

My grandfather surely was a happy-go-lucky fellow with all his whistling and crazy ideas, and so different from my practical, serious-minded grandmother, but I've wondered if these differences, in fact, made their life together viable. I've wondered if his ways – the ways that sometimes filled my grandmother with vexation – often helped keep the veil of depression from cloaking her. I give her much credit for the courage she mustered to rebuild a life alone. She moved back to BC and took that apartment near the Century House senior centre and not far from her sister's home. And for eight or nine years, she kept the darkness at bay.

Then, after Audelie's husband, Henri, died, the two sisters, both in their early eighties, moved to a lovely, modern, high-rise building – my grandmother, into a two-bedroom apartment on the eleventh floor and Audelie, into a two-bedroom apartment on the fourteenth floor. I always thought this arrangement to be quite amusing after all their years together milking cows, attempting to run away, getting married together, living near one another. But maybe all of this intimate knowledge prompted the privacy of living in separate apartments, even though they still did their shopping together, had tea in the afternoon and often played cards in the evening.

"Oh yes, I like this place very much," I remember my grandmother's voice, soft and humble as she sat primly in her rocking chair looking out the large picture window of her living room. The green tips of tall trees and blue-greys of the downtown New Westminster buildings clustered against the billows of white clouds in what could have been a prairie sky. She turned her gaze toward me, her eyes watery bright in their wonder, "You know I never live in such a nice place in all my life." These words she pushed out in the rising flare of her French-Canadian accent. "Yes, I'm very happy here."

I believe she was happy in that lovely, high-rise apartment until something happened somewhere in the deepest part of her mind, the place where memories and dreams meet, and where the convolutions of the brain, advancing in years, begin to cloud or calcify. It came on slowly. During the day she was chipper as a chickadee singing in June but with night came the snow-laden, dark clouds of December, and a reoccurring half-dream that soiled the perfection of a life victoriously lived.

"That stupid man, he keep me awake all night!" she would say, wide-eyed and fearful, "he try to come through there," pointing to the heat vent in the wall. "He want to blow hot air on me. Last night, I almost burn up!"

At first the man only invaded her dreams occasionally, and except for these nighttime disturbances she was in good health, functioning normally. But still, my mother, aunts and uncles were deeply concerned about her being on her own, and eventually, with much coaxing, my gentle natured Uncle Edward convinced her to move back to Radville where she would be closer to all she knew. He and Ernie could watch over her there; and Eva, in Regina; my mother, in Brandon; and Helen, in Stettler, Alberta; all were close enough to visit her easily and regularly. So she returned to Saskatchewan in January, the weather as cold and bleak as it had been the first time she stepped off the train from Quebec all those years ago.

Four months after she settled into a suite at a seniors' complex in Radville, my Uncle Edward died of a stroke, just as my grandfather had nineteen years earlier. Edward was only fifty-six years old.

I can't say for certain that this was the tipping point for my grandmother, nor could the doctors who saw her over the years that followed, but the visits from "that man" became more and more frequent; the knocking on walls and blowing of hot air through vents tortured her sleep. At first she complained with great vigour to everyone – family, neighbours, the landlord – the experience being so real to her. "That man, he come around again last night. This morning I think I have blisters on my legs, he blow such hot air on me." But no one could solve the problem; no one could keep him away.

So, just as she had done often over the course of her life, she took matters into her own hands. My grandmother packed up her apartment as deftly as she had so many times before and moved, and moved, and moved again in the attempt to elude her tormentor, first from Radville to Regina and when there, six more times over a period of twelve years to different parts of the city until her last apartment in the seniors' complex downtown. By then she spoke only occasionally and privately about the nighttime suffering she continued to brave, her blue eyes rimmed with tears. By then, I think, she was just trying to survive. By then, perhaps, she had been here long enough.

PHILOMÈNE'S FRIED CHICKEN IN GRAVY

1 frying chicken, cut into pieces
3 tablespoons butter
1 cup flour
Salt and pepper, to taste
Water

Skin the chicken and soak in cold water. Brown the butter in an iron pot or Dutch oven at medium high heat. In the meantime, drain the chicken and pat dry. Put all the pieces in the pot and brown on both sides. Stir in the flour, salt and pepper. Cook at medium heat for approximately 30 minutes, stirring often, making sure the mixture doesn't get too brown. Reduce heat if necessary.

Add enough water, stirring constantly, to make a nice gravy. Continue to cook slowly for approximately 30 more minutes.

Most of the directions in this recipe will look familiar. They are the same as my grandmother's fried chicken recipe, except for the cup of flour and water Philomène used to make the gravy, which stews the chicken until it almost falls off the bones.

I expect my grandmother made this dish in her later years because it comforted her. When I make it now, I find it comforts me, too.

I hear her

The harvest is all but finished in southern Saskatchewan, and it's only late August. The land is close-cropped, the brown earth showing through the stubble of grain stocks like the baldness of an old man's head after a haircut. As my mother and I drive the straight line of provincial highway 2 that connects Manitoba to its neighbouring western province, it rains off and on, sometimes in a light mist, other times in big, bold drops the size of silver dollars. We are on our way to Radville. I'm going back once again to walk the streets, drive the gravel roads around the old farmland, visit the cemetery and listen to the quiet for anything I might have missed sharing in these pages, as I feel this story coming to a close.

The wheels hum along the pavement. The traffic on this road is sparse: not many cars; a transport truck now and then; a few pickups that roll slowly onto the highway from the narrow dirt roads between the fields and then trail back off to other easements a few miles further along; a tractor; and then a combine. A monstrous, prehistoric-looking machine loaded with new technologies – a DVD player and GPS system that make the long hours in the fields more comfortable and efficient. It lumbers along hugging the road's gravel shoulder so there's room on the two-lane highway for us to pass.

I peruse the land as a captain would the sea, looking out over the great expanse and watching for subtle changes in the topography. There are many. One stretch of land swells in gentle rolls like the ocean building into waves that never quite crest, the dips thick with dense brush and topped with the reaching limbs of poplars. And then, as if the sea calms to complete quiet, another stretch lays flat as far as the eye can see, except for the occasional neatly planted square hedge of caragana bushes and pines or maples, which define solitary farmyards. Big rolls of hay dot fields along the way, which eventually will be moved with a front-end loader onto a long trailer, transported to a farm by tractor, removed via the trailer's built-in conveyor belt, and then stacked two high and two deep in long rows. From there it will be used or sold as livestock feed.

My grandparents, using long forks, used to pitch hay by hand onto a wooden flatbed rack with wheels made of iron and pulled by a team of horses. Back in the farmyard, they pitched it again into a big pile next to the barn and secured it from blowing away in the wind by criss-crossing ropes over the top, the ends of which were weighted with large pieces of metal, maybe a hook or a part from an old piece of machinery. One day, when my grandfather heaved one of the ropes over the stack, where my grandmother waited to secure it, the metal landed squarely on her head and knocked her out cold. My mother told me that when my grandmother came to, she went to the house, cold-pressed the wound until it finally stopped bleeding, put a bandage on her head and then went back out to help my grandfather finish the job.

The sky is still densely clouded but the rain has stopped as we drive into Radville and turn on to the main street. We want to have lunch at the café, the same café my grandparents frequented on Saturday evenings all those many years ago and where my mother and I had lunch with my Uncle Ernie and Aunt Betty two summers ago. But the café is closed; the family is taking a summer holiday.

"What?" I say, "Why would they close in the summer of all times?"

"Well," my mother offers, "it's probably not that busy in the summer. Everybody's out in the fields."

"Of course," I say, but I'm very disappointed. I wanted our lunch to be a little memorial feast – chicken noodle soup and toasted bacon, tomato and lettuce sandwiches – exactly what we ate with my uncle that afternoon of my last visit. I wanted to honour him in this small way because he died last spring before I could make it back here again, when we would have done our summer tour of the farms and talked about more of his old memories. I thought that if I sat at one of the Arborite tables one more time I might remember some-thing else, something important I missed from that conversation that needed to be added to these stories. I take the closed café as a sign. Its old walls are not going to be allowed to speak to me, and my uncle must have already told me everything I needed to know.

But my mother and I still stand in front of the café, wrapped in our own thoughts, just looking at it. As the sun begins to peek through the clouds, I notice a small, square plaque propped in one corner of the café's window. It lists the building's occupants since it was constructed at the turn of the century:

BonTon Barber Shop
Dr. O'Shea
Cafés: Radville, Paris, Boston, LaSalle, Glencoe, Canadian and
Radville Family Restaurant, 2nd

"The LaSalle," my mother exclaims. "Oh yes, I remember now. That's what it was called when I was little."

Well, all is not lost, I think, and then say to her, "Let's go to the cemetery."

The Radville cemetery, less than a mile west of town, sits on a small rise surrounded by wheat fields. We drive through the iron-gated entrance and inch along the narrow gravel path between crosses and bouquets of faded plastic flowers propped next to head-stones. Sunlight glimmers through the shade of ancient maple trees. The heavy grey clouds are gone, as if a giant hand suddenly swept them out of the sky; now only a few tall, white puffs tilt like melting ice cream cones.

A solid prairie breeze whips my hair around my face as I spread a red blanket next to my grandmother's grave. I think of the last fields of wheat we passed on our way here, swathed in perfect rows. Sun and wind are exactly what they need to dry the long shafts of the morning's rain so they can be combined. I smile at my own thoughts; farmers always think first in terms of the land.

A chorus of crickets chirps loudly, which seems odd at high noon, but we are quiet, my mother and I.

She sets a burlap tote bag on the blanket. It contains her "read-ings," as she calls them – a selection of inspirational books she reads from every day. They are her meditation, her way of keeping her life centred. She lowers herself carefully on hands and knees and then turns to sit with her legs straight out in front of her like a little doll. Because her knees give her trouble now and then, she says. She pulls out a book and opens it on her lap. Today she will share her readings with her mother. I wander away to give her privacy and visit my uncles' graves. From where I stand I can see her lips moving. She lifts her head and closes her eyes, face to the sky. The wind blows back the bangs of her short, white hair into a curl that looks like the crest of a small wave.

As I watch her, I am reminded of the way in which my grandmother used to whisper her rosary and of my own pen's quiet scratching on the page. And I think of how each of us found her way to some semblance of comfort in this world.

Later, I take my turn alone on the red blanket, one leg tucked beneath me, the other bent close to my chest, my chin resting on my knee, pencil in hand and my journal open before me. I close my eyes. Despite the wind, the sound of the crickets creaking is as loud as you would hear in the stillness of a coming prairie night, and for a moment I see my grandmother in the purple dusk, making her way across the yard carrying pails of milk to the house. A coal oil lamp flickers in the window as the first stars appear in the sky. I open my eyes and write, *I wonder if these crickets are a sign – a little song of communion with her …*

As the words tumble out onto the page, a cricket appears next to my foot – black and big as a quarter, the biggest, blackest cricket I've ever seen. I touch it with the eraser nub of my pencil. It leaps and lands on the headstone just beneath my grandmother's name:

Marie-Anne Lacaille
1902–2000

It disappears into the long tuffs of grass that shudder in the wind.

I feel compelled to lie down now. I close my eyes again. This time everything is quiet: the rustle of the wind in the trees, the chorus of crickets, even the sound of my own breath has stilled. I am curled up next to my grandmother, just as I would have been all those years ago, beside her on her bed, watching her sleep with her lips slightly parted and one hand loosely holding a rosary on her chest.

I hear myself say, "Is there anything else, Gramma … anything?"

I feel the sting of tears in my eyes and the deep warmth of the sun on my body. And then, I hear the creak of a single cricket loud as a bullhorn in my ear. I start to laugh, a small chuckle on the verge of a giggle.

I hear her laughter in my own.

The Rest of the Recipe Collection:

A cup of this, a half teaspoon of that

A few recipes didn't make it into the stories of this book but they are a part of the collection my mother and I mulled over in the alcove of my family room. My grandmother loved to bake and the following recipes were part of her Saturday morning repertoire.

COCOA DROP COOKIES

6 tablespoons butter
1 cup white sugar
3 eggs, well-beaten
1 tablespoon milk
2 teaspoons vanilla

2 cups flour
3 tablespoons cocoa
2 teaspoons baking powder
1/2 teaspoon salt

Cream the butter and sugar. Add in the well-beaten eggs, milk and vanilla. Add the dry ingredients and mix well. Drop by teaspoonful on to a greased cookie sheet. Bake in a preheated 375 degree oven for 10 to 12 minutes.

"These were our chocolate cookies," my mother tells me. "You know how kids love chocolate … she made them just for us kids."

CORNFLAKE COOKIES

1/4 cup cream	1/4 cup flour
1/2 cup butter	1 cup cornflakes
1 teaspoon vanilla	1 cup coconut
1 cup sugar	2 egg whites, beaten stiffly

Beat cream, butter, vanilla and sugar. Add in dry ingredients. Fold in egg whites until well mixed. Drop by teaspoonful on to a greased cookie sheet. Bake in a preheated 375 degree oven for 8 to 10 minutes.

My mother remembers eating these cookies in the summer. Knowing my grandmother, she likely used the last of a box of cornflakes to make them. And I expect she only had cornflakes around during the warm months of the year, because in the winter she made hot oatmeal or chocolate soup for breakfast.

GINGERSNAP COOKIES

1 egg	2 teaspoons baking soda
1 cup white sugar	1 tablespoon ginger
3/4 cup shortening	1 teaspoon cinnamon
1/2 cup molasses	1/2 teaspoon salt
2 cups flour	Sugar for rolling

Mix egg, sugar, shortening and molasses. Add all dry ingredients and mix to form dough. By the teaspoonful, roll into little balls by hand; then roll in white sugar. Place on a greased cookie sheet and press down balls with a fork. Bake in a preheated 375 degree oven for 10 to 12 minutes.

This gingersnap recipe is much easier to prepare than the one requiring dough-rolling that my grandmother usually made. My mother calls this the "lazy recipe" but it still makes darn good cookies for dunking in milk, and my grandmother would use it when she was short on time. I don't think she could ever be considered lazy.

BROWN COOKIES

Cookie:

1 cup brown sugar
1/2 cup butter
3 cups flour

1 tablespoon molasses
1 cup sour milk
1 teaspoon baking soda

Mix sugar, butter and flour. Add molasses. Mix baking soda with sour milk (regular milk mixed with a bit of vinegar) and stir into mixture.

Sprinkle flour on the countertop. With a rolling pin, roll out cookie dough to approximately 1/4 inch (or thinner). Cut rounds or other shapes with a cookie cutter. Place rounds on a lightly greased cookie sheet and bake in a preheated 325 degree oven for 8 to 10 minutes. Cool before adding icing.

Icing:

1 teaspoon butter
7 tablespoons milk
7 tablespoons white sugar

1 tablespoon cocoa
A bit of vanilla

Melt butter in a small pot on the stove. Add milk, sugar and cocoa. Bring to a boil and stir until mixture threads when you lift the spoon out of the pot. Add vanilla. Stir well.

Cool icing and then spread on one cookie and cover with another to make a little sandwiches.

WHITE COOKIES

Cookie:

2 eggs, well-beaten
1 cup sour cream
1 teaspoon baking soda

1 cup white sugar
1 cup butter, softened
Flour, to thicken

Mix eggs and sugar. Stir in butter, sour cream and baking soda. Add flour until dough is stiff enough to roll out to 1/4 inch thick on a floured surface. Cut into rounds with a cookie cutter. Place on a lightly greased cookie sheet and bake in a preheated 375 degree oven for 8 to 10 minutes. Watch cookies during baking as they brown very quickly. Cool.

Filling:

2 cups chopped dates   1 tablespoons brown sugar
1/4 cup water

Put ingredients in pot on the stove and cook at medium heat, stirring frequently, until smooth. Cool. Spread filling on one cookie and cover with another to make little sandwiches.

For some reason the kids weren't fond of the date filling for white cookies, so my grandmother often filled them with the chocolate icing used in the brown cookies recipe. Obviously both the brown and white cookies took more preparation time than some of the others she made, so I expect my grandmother chose only one of these for her Saturday baking list, which was a well-calculated schedule – one batch of white cookies in the oven, date filling on the stove in one pot, maybe ingredients for puffed wheat cake in another … though she was known to whip up one of those (another family favourite) in a quick ten minutes any day of the week.

PUFFED WHEAT CAKE

1 cup brown sugar   3 tablespoons cocoa, if desired
1 teaspoon vanilla   1/2 cup butter
1/2 cup light or dark corn syrup 7 or 8 cups puffed wheat

Mix all ingredients, except puffed wheat, in a pot on the stove. Bring "just" to a boil, pour over puffed wheat and mix very quickly. Immediately press mixture into a 9 inch lightly greased cake pan. Let cool before cutting.

TOMATO SOUP CAKE

1 cup white sugar   1 1/2 cups flour
1/3 cup shortening   1 teaspoon cinnamon
1 can tomato soup   1/2 teaspoon cloves
1 teaspoon baking soda   1 cup raisins

Cream sugar and shortening. Put soup in a bowl and dissolve baking soda in the soup; stir into the first mixture. Add remaining ingredients, combine and pour into a lightly greased 9 inch cake pan. Bake in a preheated 375 degree oven for 30 to 35 minutes. Let cool and spread with icing sugar icing.

This cake – "moist and very delicious" in my mother's words – was a standard on most Saturday mornings, right along side my grandmother's angel food cake and its companions, spice cake and white cake. Oh, and dream cake, too.

JELLY ROLL CAKE

4 eggs, separated
1 teaspoon vanilla
3 tablespoons cold water
1 cup white sugar
1/4 cup cornstarch

1 1/2 teaspoons baking powder
3/4 cup flour
1/4 teaspoon salt
Favourite jam or jelly, to spread

Mix egg yolks, vanilla, water and sugar. Add the rest of the dry ingredients and stir vigorously. Beat egg whites to strong stiffness and fold into mixture. Spread on a lightly greased cook sheet. Bake in a preheated 350 degree oven for approximately 25 to 30 minutes. Turn cake out on to a towel and let cool completely. Spread with jam or jelly. Roll up, using the towel as a guide.

Once again, my grandmother had a knack for making a challenging recipe seem easy. She could beat a mixture by hand with as much skill as I can with an electric appliance, which was the key to producing the springy lightness desired for this cake. Too, she knew how to delicately but deftly turn the baked cake, still in the pan, upside down on a towel. My mother tells me, it would just fall out as it cooled. No problem.

BUTTER TARTS

Pastry for a dozen tart shells
1/2 cup corn syrup
2 eggs, beaten

1/2 cup butter, softened
1 teaspoon vanilla
1 cup currents or raisins, washed

Mold pastry into muffin tins. Drizzle the corn syrup into the bottom of the cups, distributing evenly. Combine beaten eggs with softened butter and vanilla; stir in raisins or currents. Fill pastry cups to 2/3 full. Bake in a preheated 425 degree oven for 15 minutes. Let cool before serving.

If she expected company for dinner, my grandmother often served butter tarts for dessert. And, if she was making a batch of pies anyway – which could be on a Saturday or any day she had the time, usually in the early hours of the morning – a dozen tart shells filled with this sweet concoction was easy for her. Around Christmas, she often made butter tarts and cake donuts in addition to the seasonal regulars … just in case, just a little extra to have around …

CAKE DOUGHNUTS

1 pound lard	1/4 cup butter, softened
2 eggs	4 teaspoons baking powder
1 teaspoon nutmeg	1 cup milk
3/4 cups white sugar	4 cups flour
3/4 teaspoon salt	

Melt approximately 1 pound of lard in a Dutch oven or similar large cooking pot on the stove at medium high heat while preparing the dough. The lard is ready to use when you can feel the heat with your hand above the melted lard. Do not let the lard get to the "smoking" point.

Mix all ingredients to a dough-like consistency. Roll out to 1/2 inch thick on a floured surface. Cut with a doughnut cutter (has a hole in the middle). Drop dough rounds into hot lard, browning on one side and then the other. Lift out of pot with a slotted spoon and set on a towel to drain off fat. While still hot, roll in white or icing sugar.

My mother doesn't recall the following recipes from when she was a child. My Aunt Helen contributed these and said my grandmother made them often. I expect she added them to her baking list after she left the farm when there was more time to read the paper and page through magazines. But there are no clipped recipes, no ingredients and instructions scrawled in my grandmother's hand on bits of paper to verify this because, of course, she never recorded a recipe in her life. "What for?" she would say, "It's only a few things." And of course, my aunt learned how to make them because she watched.

CANDY CAKE

1 1/2 cups brown sugar   1 teaspoon vanilla
1 teaspoons baking powder   1 cup butter
4 cups oatmeal   Pinch of salt

Combine all ingredients and mix thoroughly. Press evenly to about 1 to 1 1/2 inch thick in a 9 inch greased baking pan. Bake in a preheated 375 degree oven for 15 to 25 minutes.

OATMEAL CAKE

Part one:

1 1/2 cups boiling water   1 teaspoon salt
1 cup rolled oats   1 1/2 cups flour
1 cup brown sugar   1 teaspoon baking soda
1/2 cup shortening   1 cup white sugar
2 eggs   1 teaspoon cinnamon

Pour water over oats and let stand until cool. Cream shortening and sugar, and beat in eggs. Mix in the rest of the ingredients. Pour batter into a 9 inch lightly greased cake pan.

Part two:

6 tablespoons butter
1 cup coconut
2/3 cup brown sugar
1/4 cup cream or milk

Mix all ingredients, then spread on top of cake batter. Bake until brown, in a preheated 350 degree oven for approximately 30 minutes. Let cake cool. Cut into serving squares and top with caramel icing (recipe below).

Icing:

3/4 cup brown sugar
4 1/2 teaspoons cream
2 1/2 teaspoons butter
1 teaspoon vanilla

Mix sugar, butter and cream in a pot on the stove. Boil for 1 1/2 minutes. Add vanilla and beat well. Drizzle over servings of oatmeal cake.

PEANUT BUTTER CAKE

1/2 cup shortening
1 1/2 cups brown sugar
2 eggs
1/2 cup peanut butter
2/3 cup milk

1/2 teaspoon vanilla
1/2 teaspoon baking powder
1 1/2 cups flour
1/2 teaspoon salt

Combine shortening, sugar and eggs. Stir in milk, vanilla and peanut butter. Add the dry ingredients and mix well. Pour batter into a lightly greased 9 inch cake pan. Bake in a preheated 350 degree oven for 30 minutes.

CHOCOLATE WALNUT CAKE

2 squares of baking chocolate
2 eggs
1 cup brown sugar
1/2 cup butter
1 teaspoon vanilla

1/2 teaspoon baking powder
3/4 cup flour
1 teaspoon salt
1 cup walnuts, chopped

Melt chocolate in a double boiler on the stove. In the meantime, mix eggs, butter, sugar and vanilla. Add the melted chocolate and stir. Add the dry ingredients and walnuts, and mix well. Pour into a lightly greased 9 inch cake pan. Bake in a preheated 375 degree oven for approximately 30 minutes.

Acknowledgements

This book has been a labour of love. Its purpose is to pay tribute to my dear grandmother and also to many other women of the early Twentieth Century, whose journeys on this earth were both arduous and victorious.

First and foremost I must thank my mother, Florence Mazer, who patiently walked the terrain of her memories many, many times over to help flesh out the stories about my grandmother, and who continues to carry on her mother's tradition of living fully, with tenacity and verve. And to all the other beautiful women in my life – especially my sisters, Elaine and Sylvia – who do the same; they form the inspiration that gives me the resilience to continue to follow my passion.

My Aunt Helen Wells offered important story details and several recipes for the collection. Uncle Ernie, before he passed away, opened a window into my grandmother's world that this book could not do without, and Aunt Betty surprised me with the windfall of two recipes actually written in my grandmother's hand. My mother's cousin, Andrea Riviere, contributed terrific anecdotes, as well.

I am extremely grateful to Julien Fradette for compiling the 1984 Fradette family genealogy, which provided important insights and historical information, including Ferdinand's homestead document. I must also thank the Radville Laurier Historical Society for their comprehensive chronicle of the town, its residents and surrounding area; and also to the good folks at the Deep South Pioneer Museum in Ogema, Saskatchewan. Their dedication to preserving the past offered me viewings of everything from threshers and binders to McClary stoves, Singer sewing machines and to the kind of wooden crates my grandmother used to transport her eggs to Radville for sale. And thanks to my cousin Sharon Michelau for the photos of my grandmother's famous iron pot, which is in her safekeeping.

I would like to acknowledge Rachel Manley for encouraging the first seeds of this story, and offer special thanks to Jane Brox for her guidance in helping me shape the thesis that eventually turned into *The Work of Her Hands*. And also to my friend and colleague, Celia Jeffries, who serendipitously bumped into Noelle Allen at a writers' conference and then had the brilliant idea of introducing us. Along with Noelle, many thanks go to Lindsay Hodder and Ashley Hisson from Wolsak and Wynn for their devotion to every aspect of this book.

I save my most immeasurable gratitude for my sons Mitchell and Daniel – the heart of my existence – and my ever-loyal, husband and best friend, Michael, who provide the haven that is our family to pursue my dreams.

Recipe Index